WK INTERACT

EXTERIOR ACT 2 INTERIOR

I want to thank...

Yael Reich
for supporting me during the most difficult times and for being the love of my life.

My brother Franck Desplanques
who gave me the challenge that nothing is impossible.

My parents and my grandparents
for their love.

Dan
for all the different characters. Without him none of this motion could be done.

Robert Christensen
for his help and for filming me on each project for 12 years.

Christopher Lee
for giving me the best of his martial art.

Harry Jumonji 100% skate
for believing in me and for a great collaboration.

Max Osterweis
for a 14 years relationship.

Isabel Kirsch
for introducing me to the publisher and for finding the right words.

Louis Yoh
for lending me his MV for more than 2 months.

Michael and Dominick Regina
for letting me use their property and always helping me.

Gregoire Puzenat
for being one of my first models and a great friend.

Aurelio Garcia
for the best time traveling and helping me to set up my illegal work on billboards.

Becky
for being so sexy.

Jessica Goolke
for all her patience with teaching how to speak English.

Christ Apple
for giving me the great opening at my store studio 101.

Liza
for the sexy roller blade.

Young Kim
for collaborating at my opening.

Graig
for the roller blade motion on Broadway.

Patrick Muligan
for helping me in the last 2 years and for photographing.

Jim
for the power muscle.

Taly Malka
for setting up my web site and for teaching me to work on the computer.

Ruthard Miksch
for the best spy.

My Aureilio
for helping me with my first illegal billboard in France 19 years ago.

Take :
for the motion of urban street and for assisting me in the last 2 years.

And thanks to all the people living in NYC and the city itself for giving me the opportunity to challenge myself.

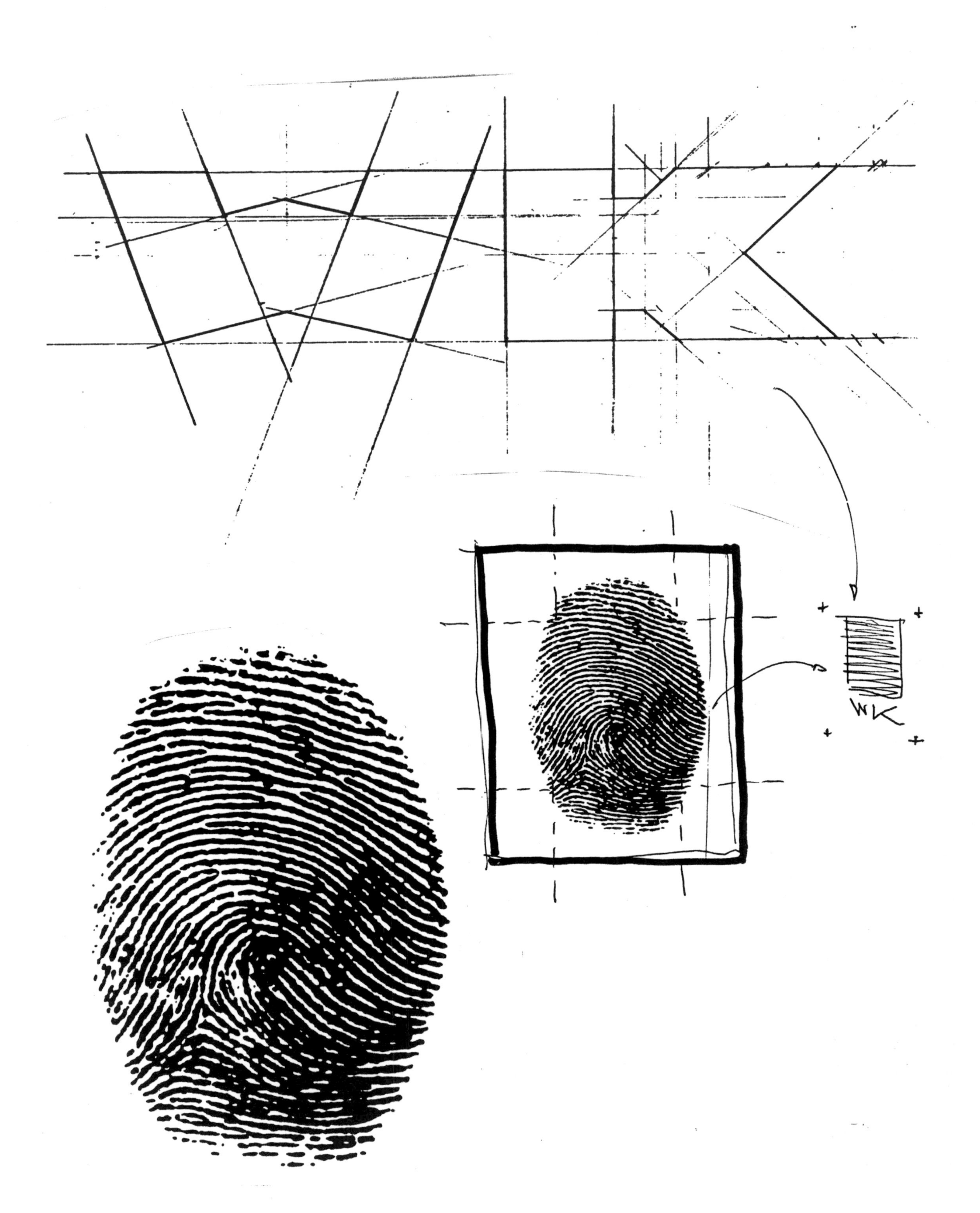
WK

63480#NY
4
B-028
WK 2700342
139

R-027-079-A
1108257
NEW YORK USA
0359
4
HEADACHE
KINKY

A conversation with WK interact

WK Interact is an urban artist living in New York City, whose street art started appearing there in the early 1990s. Amazing examples of his striking imagery are exhibited on the streets of downtown Manhattan; his most renowned artworks are undoubtedly the black and white murals at the corner of Lafayette and Prince Street in East SoHo.
Originally from the picturesque village of Saint Paul de Vence in the south of France, WK moved to New York at the young age of 18 many years ago. After struggling hard to make a living in the big city while pursuing his painting projects, he finally gained recognition as an artist approximately ten years later. WK has exhibited in Germany, Spain, UK, Italy, Japan, Australia and Denmark. The following interview took place in December 2004.

1. What role did art play in your childhood?

I started drawing when I was 8 years old. Both of my parents are interior designers, and I spent a lot of time observing and imitating my father. To keep me busy while he was painting one day, he gave me a little piece of canvas and I replicated one of his paintings. He subsequently gave me a drawing book that was almost bigger than me. And in the beginning I made only little drawings on those huge pages while we worked in his amazing office at the large drawing table. This is how I started. I kept drawing and drawing, and that period turned out to be a very important stage for me. It was a very happy one as well. And so in school I was always the kid making sketches and drawing faces. It was always very natural for me to have charcoal or a pencil in my pocket.

2. Do you have any formal training in art?

When I was sixteen years old I attended an after school program at Beaux Arts in Nice. It was a free school for talented kids; if you were good they would keep you. At art school I learned something interesting: I was accustomed to drawing while seated at a table, but I was taught how to draw standing up. I enjoyed drawing human figures, working with clay and generally appreciated being acquainted with other disciplines within the realm of art. I dropped out of school when I was eighteen years old to attend a school for interior design, graphic design and architecture. There I discovered that I had a talent for drawing three dimensional spaces, something that had always interested me. I also focused on outlines of objects as well as sketches with varied shadow depictions. Eventually I found that I had no trouble conveying the structures of hands or even eyes. At that point my drawings consisted primarily of three-dimensional human figures, and they all had to do with motion.

3. When did you become fascinated by the motion of the human body?

The fascination was always there, but I really started to get into it in high school. There were a lot of dance schools in the area and I would go to one and asked if it was possible to sketch the dancers. I spent all my free time at dance schools for a whole year. My interest was less focused on an attempt to draw humans than it was on my efforts to capture the motion of leaping dancers. At the time it seemed nearly impossible to sketch a line of the jumping human form because I had to summarize a two-second sequence within the context of a single line. I was unaware of my intense desire to understand motion in that respect, but I was already quite driven with regard to moving toward that end. For me everything was about speed and motion. One day I was experimenting with a new technique. I took one of my pictures and stretched it in a Xerox machine. I also employed several different layers of other pictures. The result was exactly what I wanted and was worthy of emulation. I was mesmerized by the creation of some kind of industrial motion. It was half industrial and half hand drawing. And when I got the piece right, I wanted to bring it to the street. But in real size and in three dimensions. I figured the best way to display the motion of a person running down the street was to use a street corner. In essence, for me, it was never about doing something on the street, but it was simply about investigating the potential of my concept.

4. How would you characterize your evolution as a street artist?

I started working on the street not because I wanted to be a street artist, but because I found the ideal stage to create speed and three-dimensional motion in urban architecture. When I began experimenting with the urban scenario, I was entirely unaware of what other people had done before me. I didn't realize how many different artists had already been working in the streets. I started doing street art in Nice, in the south of France, and in a single night I did eight different pieces in various locations. Nice was not exactly the best place to do urban street art - not because it was dangerous - it just didn't seem to be an adequate way to reach people. It was not the right the time for street art in Nice, and the streets were quickly cleaned up after the work was finished. One day I met with a well-known art critic, and when she saw pictures of my work on the street she compared me to other artists who were unknown to me. So I went to the library to look up these artists, and I found information on other artists who, like me, were experimenting with different approaches to capturing figures in motion with respect to graphics and painting. I also realized that none of those artists employed my simple technique to create motion. That was exciting. I was motivated to work more intensely and more regularly on new projects.

I began to paint on billboards first in France and then in London. Increasingly I began committing my work to paper as well. My work expanded into the realm of photography as I began taking experimental pictures of a friend in motion. It all continued to be a personal endeavor, one disassociated from a desire to have people care about my work. It was purely me doing my thing, unrelated to an art form or movement.

5. So you didn't choose the street as a means to public recognition or fame?

Not at all. It was just something I was driven to do and I had always been captivated by inner-city street culture and urban architecture. I have this archaeological tendency to observe details on the street, and I am constantly looking to find inspiring objects. I like both the energy emanating from the street as well as the freedom it represents. In no way I was thinking that I was making any sense or that I was going to be recognized for this type of work. Back then I was still making good money as a storyboard artist and interior set designer. I kind of did the street art on the side. It was nothing spectacular and didn't cost me much. It was simply painting on paper, cutting it and applying it to the right locations. So from there I decided to go to New York. It seemed like the perfect city for what I wanted to do, and I can say that 99% of my current work is based on my experience here in New York. When I came to New York I immediately discovered that I had to adjust to the scale of the city. I felt the need to draw my pictures 200 times bigger. It was a great challenge.

6. As an adolescent were there any artists that you considered heroes or whose work greatly influenced you?

I didn't really have a hero. The artists I admired included Giacometti, Egon Schiele, Daniel Spoerri, Tinguely, Tapies, Beuys, Basquiat, Gordon Matta, Clark, Calder, Van Lieshout, and Niki de St Phalle. The sculptor and painter, Giacometti as an example, was influential in his use shadow and lines. As a seventeen year old teenager, I discovered the graffiti world. I became aware of graffiti artists like Mode 2, Futura, Lee, Lokiss and the BBC crew without knowing that ten years later I would meet them personally.

7. How did you end up in New York, and what were your first years like?

I came to New York for the first time when I was sixteen. The city had an incredible impact on me. Two years later I decided to return to New York with the singular idea of focusing on my personal work. I didn't know

anyone and I didn't speak any English.
My attempts to find work as an interior designer were very disappointing. I had a meeting with an architect and interior designer. After showing them my books and talking for a while the architect told me that my book was great. Then he asked me if I spoke English. When I told him that I did not, he closed my book said: "There is nothing for you to do here in the States. You better leave again." I was kind of disillusioned but he was right. How could I articulate what I was doing without speaking the language? For about a year and a half I survived in New York by doing regular jobs as a painter and carpenter. All the handcraft skills I had acquired in France actually helped me pay my rent and purchase food.

8. While you were living on the Lower East Side, how did you get involved with the New York street scene?

I was living on Houston Street between Avenue A and B. It's funny and a bit weird how I encountered the artists I had always wanted to meet. I was never trying to get close to them. It just happened by accident. I always wanted to meet Richard Hambleton, a street artist who was big in the early 80s. Back then this guy used to do images of life-sized human shadows, and his stuff totally intrigued me. My only experience with his work was a small picture I saw in a book. It stuck with me though, and I was eager to meet him. Two years later in the park across the street from where I live, I saw someone from the back. He wasn't painting or anything but I knew it was Richard. It's one of the weirdest things that has happened to me in my life. I stopped and ask him for his name. He turned around and went like "Yeah, what do you want?" I had been looking for him for a long time. Everybody told me he was dead because he had been using a lot of drugs and had disappeared for a while, but he was actually living right across the street from me. It's strange how destiny arranged our meeting when I least expected it. A similar thing happened when I met Futura and Mode 2. It was more destiny or coincidence than anything else. All these people were and are still quite important. They have been important to me from the beginning because of their work with the spray can and their significance for the global graffiti culture. Although their work was different than mine, I was always familiar with their scene. I paid attention to what they were doing because they started on the streets as well.

9. Did you ever go around tagging walls?

No, I was never interested in tagging walls with my name or symbols related to my life.

Preparations for street bombing

I always wanted to represent something alive, to tell a story that has happened on a street corner with some kind of motion. I wanted to achieve the effect of action to create something sarcastic, or crazy, something that produced strong emotions like fear or laughter. It was all about being in New York and representing New York the way I experienced it.

10. How would you describe what you do? Would you call it graphic art?

It's a mix of storyboard illustration, graphic art and photography. It's also architecture and interior design. It's a lot of things together.
I call it interactive urban street art. And it took me twenty years to come up with the concept. My intention is to create something inconclusive, something without a clear ending so that you have to imagine a negative or positive conclusion yourself. I try to free the image from the frame. I hate being limited by frames. The streets of New York are perfect for my work, and I prefer to use corners and uneven surfaces instead of flat clean walls. When I work with paper and glue, I cut the image to size so that it fits exactly on the background and appears flat.

11. Why is it that you rarely work with color?

When I started I wanted to come up with something very minimalist and very simple in order to create a strong effect. I also didn't have any money. And at the time I painted buildings for work. I used to consolidate the leftover buckets of white paint, and then I'd buy a gallon of acrylic black to keep my expenses minimal. The idea was that I wanted people to directly experience the motion in the artwork instead of offering too much information with color. Earlier I had painted in full color. With full color you almost have to sit down and study the image, but with black and white you can pass by the image in a car or on a bicycle and just capture the motion. As the elements compromise the integrity of the painting, it gets better. The perfect black and white painting becomes more alive the longer it is exposed to the street; the environment adds to the manipulation the object. For those who rush by, the sequence of images becomes a flipbook-like effect. What I love most about it is that the wall looks different depending on the time of day, the weather, traffic, perspective, and the speed of the viewer. The interaction between various factors that make up a street corner in New York lends the work a sense of completeness.

Williamsburg Bridge 1994

12. Interaction with street life is a significant part of your work. How do you feel about showing your art in an inside space such as a gallery? Aren't you sacrificing the effect you're getting on the outside?

I am still doing quite a lot of indoor and outdoor projects. However, I still believe that the most difficult thing to do is to isolate "life" and commit it to canvas. It's extremely hard, and I don't think I'll ever stop working on the street. I will always be doing some installation outside or at the very least my work will be inspired by the street. I am very sensitive to the street, to the people and how they view me. I am aware of my personal relationship with the street and of the fact that these people have informed my identity. I don't consider myself talented or artistic. If I consider my work, I feel that it is largely informed by the audience's response to my prior work. In the past, especially in New York, there was no reason to do anything for free out on the street. It is still a little bit like that. Life in New York is too expensive to be doing unpaid work. I did it and it was purely my own challenge. I would single out a wall or a corner and apply something to it, but at the same time I feared that it might be impossible to do by myself. I needed a scaffolding to get way up there. But I would do it anyway and incredibly exhaust myself working non-stop for 48 hours without even eating.

13. How do you find locations? What are the criteria for your to site selection?

I look around, find the best location and create a story for the location. Only certain places are capable of telling a story: a garbage deposit, a public phone or a doorway. The cleaner the wall, the less I am interested. I try not to work over tags on walls. That's part of the street's beauty, and I don't want to take over the whole place. When I arrived in New York, I became immediately aware of its size and understood the challenge of trying to figure out which neighborhood would be most suitable for my work. I began on the Upper West Side. I scoured nearly 20 blocks a day. I did the entire Upper West Side, Midtown, and then the East Side up to the 70s. After one month making sketches, going corner by corner and location by location, I finally went back to where I lived and determined that my downtown neighborhood, a 20 block area, was most appropriate for my work. Back then the Lower East Side and SoHo were dying. They were in certain decline. Working in those environments was the wrong direction for most artists. I got very lucky and the situation turned to my advantage. That happened to me a lot. I'd find a location that nobody was interested in, and a couple of years later the spot became the happening center of the city.

14. Some of your most legendary pieces covered the huge wall on Lafayette and Prince. How did you get permission to paint there?

I found the location very appealing, but the first job I did there was completely destroyed by someone the next day. I was very disappointed because I didn't even have a photo of it. A week later I went to see the superintendent of the building, showed him a sketch and asked if I could paint on the wall. He told me it was impossible. I was very persistent and eventually arranged to meet the owner of the building to present my idea. He asked me how much this was going to cost him, and I said it wouldn't cost him anything. So he looked at me and said: "If you are stupid enough to paint my wall for nothing it's fine," and that if I could get the job done in two days he would let me do the rest of the building. I went back the same night and worked like crazy the whole night through applying some base color. Since I didn't have any funding, I used some paint that I had found on the street. I wasn't lucky with the weather as it was rained all night. The next day at noon, the owner came by to check on me. He was a very sweet guy but a really tough one. He was not the kind of guy who would give anything away for no reason. When he came to visit me, I was standing under a shelter waiting for the rain to stop. The next time he came by it was 1AM in the morning. And when he realized I was still there doing my thing, he told me that my desire to paint there was incredible and that he had been joking about the two-day time limit. He said that he felt a little bit guilty because he knew I was never going to finish in such a short time period. I ended up having an incredible relationship with this man. His name was Michael Regina. After he passed away, his son Dominick told me that before his father died he had told him to always look out for me. He said he had believed so much in me. The son liked my work even better than his father had, and he told me that I could do whatever I wanted so I'd keep coming back to paint on this building. I am fortunate to have such a friendly relationship with this family. I'm also fortunate to have the best corner in the city. It is an amazing corner, an open space that you can see from all angles. It is from this corner that everything started. Every two or three years I paint something new, tell a different story. The first work was a little businessman on the run. Then there was a sexy girl jumping from the top of the building. After that I painted the laughing head of black super model Alec Wek. Next I painted Robert all tied up, desperately trying to break free. Then the terrorists running around, then beautiful Yael throwing her head from side to side, and then the martial arts guy. I continued some of the thematic material with something funny on different portions of the

Williamsburg Bridge 1994

wall. You saw the businessman running, then the killer running after the businessman, and after the killer vanished the business guy was under attack by the martial arts guy. This location is magic. Much later I found out that Basquiat, who I admire a lot, was living on this corner and that Keith Haring used to do a lot of drawing on the same street.

15. Did you ever get arrested?

Not really. A couple of times the cops came by but they knew my work, and they were very nice to me. They just said: "Why don't you go somewhere else where we're not going to see you?" And also, being so active on the street I got to know all the homeless in my area. I had a deal with them. I'd give them food and they would watch out for me. But generally I never expected anyone to help me. I was a survivor, someone who didn't need much and someone who got excited discovering things and meeting interesting people. Painting on the street can be very difficult because some people like your stuff and some people don't. So you have to be diplomatic and extremely open to different personalities. You also have to be very social and patient. I experienced so many things with people on the streets of New York. People would bring me food and wait to speak with me. Some people wanted to give me money. So many people came to talk to me that I felt very special. This would never happen in my country. The people living in New York were so incredibly good to me. They were impressed seeing one person doing a big wall with no assistance in freezing cold weather. In this city, if they see you struggling for some reason, they see power in your work. When they see activity they think, "OK, he's going somewhere." They sense positive effort, and they're feeling that and they want to give you something in return.

16. You're very good with people, but in the end you're a lone warrior...

At the time I could not expect to ask anybody for help if I was not paying for it. If you subject yourself to adverse circumstances, you have to face it and handle it by yourself. Some people can get really depressed when things get difficult. For me my situation gave me strength. The more I struggled the more motivated I became to accomplish something. I was always busy seeking a bigger, more challenging location. I am completely addicted to the challenge of doing many things in only one day. And I didn't want to repeatedly paint the same image. Each location required the appropriate concept for which I had to create the right material.

Preparation and first illegal billboard screen, Nice 1989 • Billboard screen mounted at railway track, Nice

AVENIR
W.K
La maison de Johnnie Walker
RUE
REINE JEANNE

W.K

Preparation and first illegal installation on billboard, Nice 1989

It was all about just doing it and seeing how lucky you can get when you have no one to help you. You could compare it to somebody climbing a crazy mountain for no reason. You could easily take a helicopter to get to the top, but a lot of things happen while you're climbing. I make a little sketch and I say, "OK, you have to do it now." And usually I never get off the ladder until I finish with my last drop of paint. Then I sit down to look at my work and to criticize its size, scale, and conveyance of intended motion.

17. There are many steps from the initial idea to the finished painting. Could you describe your creative process?

For me, location dictates the project and the story behind it. Once I find a suitable spot for a piece, I create a storyboard that matches the particular wall and street. Next I think of the person who would be the right model for the project at hand. The figures on my paintings are all real people: So far I used skater, kung-fu-master, boxer, rock climber, basket ball player and many others. I carefully consider whom I want to paint and I become intensively involved with this person. When I am working with a skater, I turn into a skater and I am visually incredibly inspired by the stunts you can do with a piece of wood on wheels. During elaborate studio sessions, I take pictures of the model reproducing specific motion sequences. The greatest difficulty is to depict motion in stillness. Only intensive engagement with the sport or activity of the model allows me to capture the desired effect of motion. The most important thing for me is to consider from where the image originates and why the person is collaborating with me. If I chose an image from a magazine to model my work on, I could never achieve the same effect. I always try to be part of my work. The fact that I go by the pseudonym WK allows me to de-emphasize my role within the art. I forget my origins, my home and who I am. I take on a new identity. I become a part of the concept, which includes architecture, street life, the challenge of an extreme sport, and many other elements.

18. In the last five years your career got a boost and you have been increasingly in demand. What were the milestone projects for this period?

In the last five years, I was given the chance to work on a range of quiet incredible projects: Amongst others I worked with Yamaha, Burton, with BMW and Yohji Yamamoto. I had the opportunity to go to Japan to do four large exhibitions. All these things happened in five years and I have been working on two to three major projects every year. This winter I went to Paris to design twelve windows of the Galleries Lafayette storefront. I came

Garagedoor on Ludlow St

forward with the proposal to paint inside the attached Metro station. The idea was to visually connect the subway with the department store and to create a tunnel or a spiral motion that drives the energy from the outside to the inside of the store. In Paris thousands of people from different cultures are using the subway system. I considered the location and I wanted to produce something positive, not necessarily a sequence of people killing each other. I always try to make sense of what type of motion I apply.

19. Concerning your cooperation with commercial brands, how do you define your role in the development of a project or a campaign?

Most of the time when a sponsor is knocking on my door, they are not really sure what to do with me and so I usually come up with a full concept that applies to them in a constructive and artistic way. I allow myself to be inspired by what a company does but I also try to look at them from a different angle. I take an object - a Burton snowboard for example - and instead of focusing solely on the snowboard, I ask Burton to contact Yamaha to get a snow mobile. In conjunction with the snow mobile the snowboard becomes an object that enables rescuing people from otherwise inaccessible areas. The story is no longer about just the snowboard but also about who is using it and what is happening to it. It is a very aesthetic, practical and futuristic way to look at things. My aspiration is not to impose my image and artwork upon a marketing project, but to find an approach how to conceptually upgrade an object and thus make it art. I try to collaborate, give a sponsor what they wish my work should achieve and get them excited. I want to have an impact on the client, the product, whilst touching the people who are buying it. Demanding too much from your own image may take the focus away from the purpose. Of course you have to the best artwork to go with the product, but in the end the marketing setup is counting more than the quality of the artist.

20. Many of your projects go beyond visual art. They could be defined as street performances in which every related object and detail has been crafted by yourself. Like the propaganda project you did in 2003...

It is true that I do not only focus on projects that portray motion. Within the context of the urban environment, the city and its inhabitants, I develop concepts of interaction that could range from a visual language to a political statement.

The propaganda project was initiated years ago when I found a few metal newspaper boxes, the ones that used to line the corners of midtown Manhattan and from which you could draw a newspaper for a few cents. I wanted to utilize the boxes for some time, but just painting on them was not enough. There had to be a concept surrounding the boxes. The figure that I painted on the boxes is the New York City angst man, who is tied up and is desperately trying to break free. With these boxes I went out into the city, dressed in an all-white outfit that said, "Interact now", and set up propaganda stands in different locations: Times Square, Union Square, basically all of New York City's hectic spots. Principally, the idea was to sell spray cans instead of newspapers. The objective was not to sell, but to initiate disgruntled New Yorkers to reach for spray cans instead of writing letters or screaming into the phone. People could choose between black or white, depending on what background they wanted to write on. There was barely any reaction; even the cops let me be. The "interact" in my name stands for that part of me that is entirely concerned with things that simultaneously influence one another. And by the way, I chose my name WK Interact long before the interactive media boom.

21. Then there are the urban camouflage projects that only marginally touch the subject of painting. You have designed outfits and equipment of generic NYC characters, which enable the wearer to perfectly blend into the environment. Do you camouflage yourself to access places and do things you normally couldn't do?

There is definitely some sarcastic and comical aspect to this, but I do like the effectiveness and the practical way of how I can become un-seen and I wanted to test out how far I can go. Fixated with street art – most of which is illegal - I started to carefully observe the different worlds that make up the city. What exactly is happening in Uptown, Downtown, Wall Street or Chinatown during night and day? Who are the prevailing characters? On Wall Street there are a lot of business guys so I became a businessman carrying a suitcase. I roamed Chinatown as a disabled person, some guy in a wheelchair who is asking people for change - the level of the wheelchair is perfect to tag on cars. Through these experiences I found myself blending into the environment and subsequently not being targeted as a street artist. Clusters of black plastic bags filled with garbage are a predominant element in Manhattan, so I created an outfit based on garbage bags. Every year during fashion week thousands of media people are coming into the

city. With the right attire nobody suspects you're a tagger. Carrying a fake press card and a bunch of cameras permitted me to freely cascade through restricted areas camouflaged as a typical fashion week photographer. The goal is to enable the ultimate assimilation to any situation or location. If I resided in another region of the world, I would design camouflages equivalent to the local stereotypes. I took the whole idea from spying. To bomb or tag walls is one thing, but to design and wear different outfits and tactically act as another person elevates it to another level. This kind of illegality inspires me. It's an adrenaline rush, a lot of fun and such an important portion of my work. And certainly it prevents me from getting arrested.

22. One time you took it as far as living on the street like a homeless person for a while. What was that all about?

I camped out on the street in winter for a couple of weeks as Mr. Camo. This guy symbolizes sheer survival and green is his color. One reason why he is wearing green army clothes is because it is an inexpensive and practical way to dress for a man with his lifestyle. More importantly the green outfit helps him to blend into his environment and to hide from the police as sleeping on the street is an illegal act. He likes to hang out in parks. Surrounding himself with green he becomes a part of it and turns invisible. Living on the street Mr. Camo survives by finding and recycling objects. I would carry a collection of objects with me in a box and these were all the belongings Mr. Camo had. I think what motivated me to be Mr. Camo was that 17 years ago I was forced to sleep on the street and I wanted to remember how it was. What this whole homeless survival experience does to you is fascinating! You learn something very special and it changes you in a way that you start looking at things very differently. You become very alert and very aware of your surroundings and you know exactly how to react in any situation. By sleeping outside on the boardwalk you can feel the street so much stronger, you feel like you actually own the street. This allowed me to do things that other people wouldn't be able to do.

23. A part of what you do is to manipulate random objects that you find on the street. You also invent new things or intelligently optimize tools so they suit your purpose better.

I collect objects that seem worthless to some people, but when you put them together, recycle them or carry them around like Mr. Camo, they can turn into treasures.

Truck utilities for large quantities of posters

Some objects have no value at all, however they are important assets to the homeless. There is this Chinese homeless man who I photographed. He is sitting there mounting up all these bags around him except in the bags there is nothing but old newspaper. For him these bags serve a very important purpose: They function as a wall to shelter him from the cold.
The tools that go with my different outfits have been designed for both, practical and aesthetical reasons. I like to apply my personal color or style to objects, then it is the accumulation of a certain type of objects that makes it significant. If you look at all of them combined they have a continuation, they fit together. To expose myself as a person is not really my thing. I rather present myself by accumulating and exhibiting the objects I manipulated in one space. You get the effect that everything belongs to one and the same person in its individual style.

24. You don't see yourself only as a painter. What are you then? A graphic artist, architect, innovator or performance artist?

I am definitely a painter: I paint oil; I can paint in 3D and in color but I don't consider myself as a painter. Sure, I use a brush and I am painting a motion on canvas but for me painting is a totally different thing. I sketch graphic illustrations not drawings. Because a great part of my work is based on the street you could perceive it as installation and adaptation of a concept that might have been initiated with a sketch. I am also good at package and architectural design, landscaping and at interacting with objects. So why should I be called an artist or a painter when it is actually not what I am doing? Maybe it's a new generation? Maybe people call us artists, but on my journeys I have seen many incredible and talented artists that I cannot compare myself to. It is true that people know me because I have been featured in different magazines and fashion editorials. My work has been displayed on the streets of New York for so many years that it has been multiplied and further distributed by being photographed on countless occasions. However there are other people out there who are extremely good, who studied for many years but who will be unknown because they never get this kind of exposure.

25. How much of a factor has the location New York been to your success?

At the time I chose New York as my base because I thought the city was perfect for the imagery I wanted to create on the street. During this instance I completely forgot the aspect of the size of the city, that New York is the biggest multicultural metropolis of the world. For me it was like a village, I spent most of my time on the street and rode my bike from one corner to the next doing my thing. I didn't realize that the effect you're getting here is a hundred times bigger than anywhere else. I truly have to thank New York and the people of New York for everything I have achieved.
Diversity is the main contributor to New York culture; the gigantesque buildings, this incredible energy emerging from the ground of New York, the fact that everything is open 24 hours and that you have a freedom here, which you cannot find anywhere else. Not just freedom for an artist, but also sexual freedom, racial freedom and freedom of individual expression. New York is for anyone who wants to realize their dreams and achieve something for them self. The same way New York can bring out the best in someone it can bring out the worst. It's the city of harsh extremes.

26. What is coming next? What are your future plans?

I am a little bit bored with black and white and motion. The flat image was never so important to me. When I started to open my store and gallery I rediscovered the object. In a way that the 3-dimensional aspect of objects has always been a means for me to create motion. I glue an image around a street corner to make the motion go around, but these days it is difficult to find the right corner. So what I increasingly like to do is painting on objects to create this multidimensional effect. The fact that objects are moveable is another intriguing feature. I am striving to apply an image to larger objects like a boat, a submarine or a plane, or paint on rocks by the sea. There are so many ways of creating motion. I am also adding more complexity to my work showing multiple motions instead of one. Life has changed in New York. The city is getting cleaner and law enforcement more serious. When I am unable to do something out on the street, I will take objects from the streets to reassemble and recycle them: Metal, wood or even a plant.

27. What would your advice be to aspiring artists?

Work hard! Don't expect to get somewhere only counting on your talent. You really need to work extremely hard; not to produce a lot but to find quality in your work. It always takes a certain time. For example if you decide to build a table with some tools you're not going to be able to do so until you get a sense for the type of wood you're using and until you learn how to work with the tools. Anything you do takes time. The beauty of it is not what you achieve but it's actually the work itself. Whatever you do it shouldn't be for money and fame but to prove something to yourself. Patience is the key. Never expect things to happen too quickly and don't wait for other people to help you. When I did the major wall on Prince and Lafayette there was no feedback for five years, not even one article and nobody knew who I was. It would have been easy to add a web address or a phone number, but I wanted people to figure out by themselves who I am. I only wanted the right people to find me. I told the owner of the house not to give my information to anyone but to have people drop their card with him so I could get in touch with them. A huge wall like this, noticed by so many people appears to be commercial, but in reality it was the opposite.

NO CREDIT
CARDS
ACCEPTED!
FAT
CAT.
WK04

NYC struggle: Tied up by stress and survival angst 1997 (top) • Wallstreet Headache (bottom left) • Sexy Beast (bottom right)

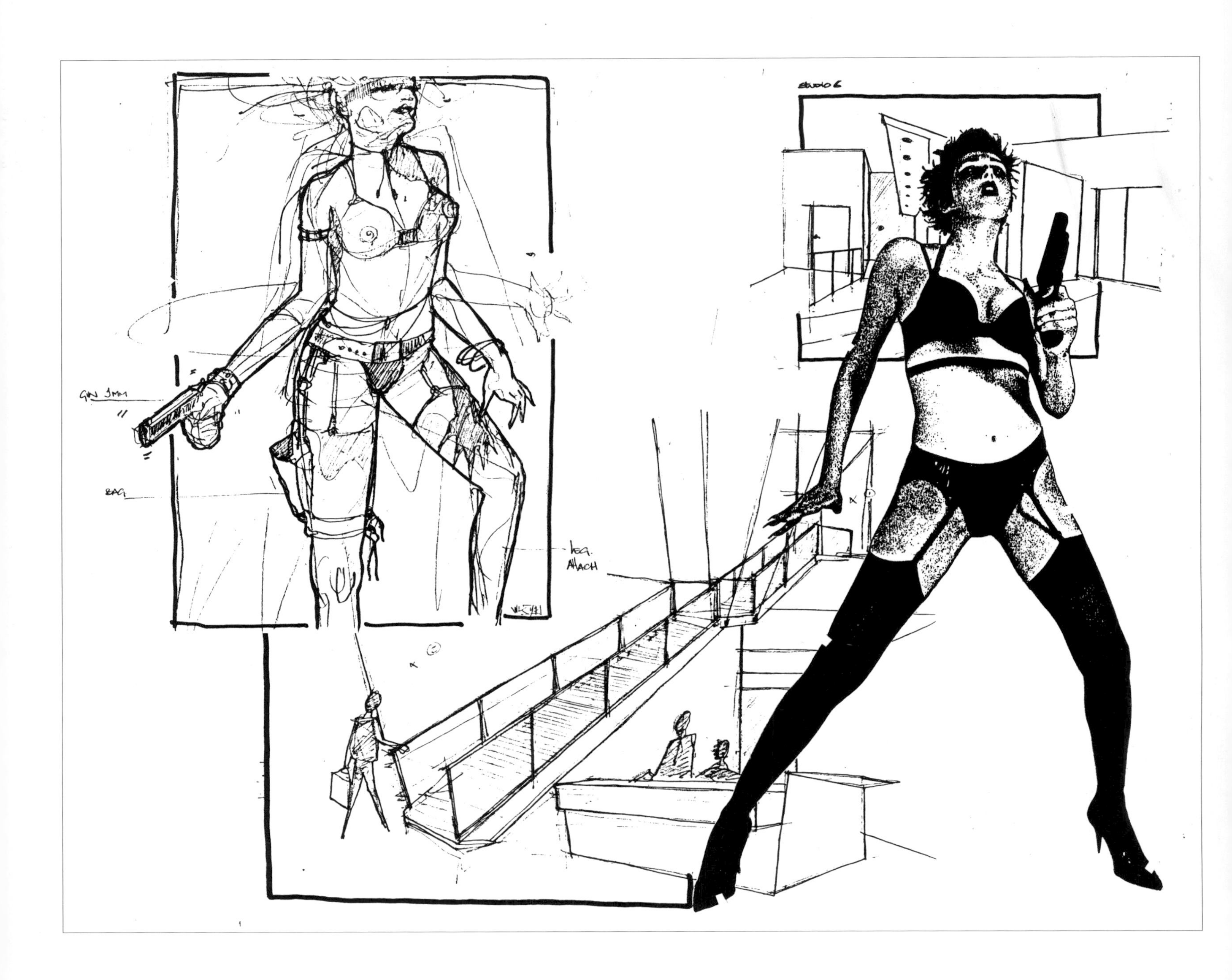

Piers 54 1998 (top) • Sweet Dream (bottom left) • Sexy Blades (bottom right)

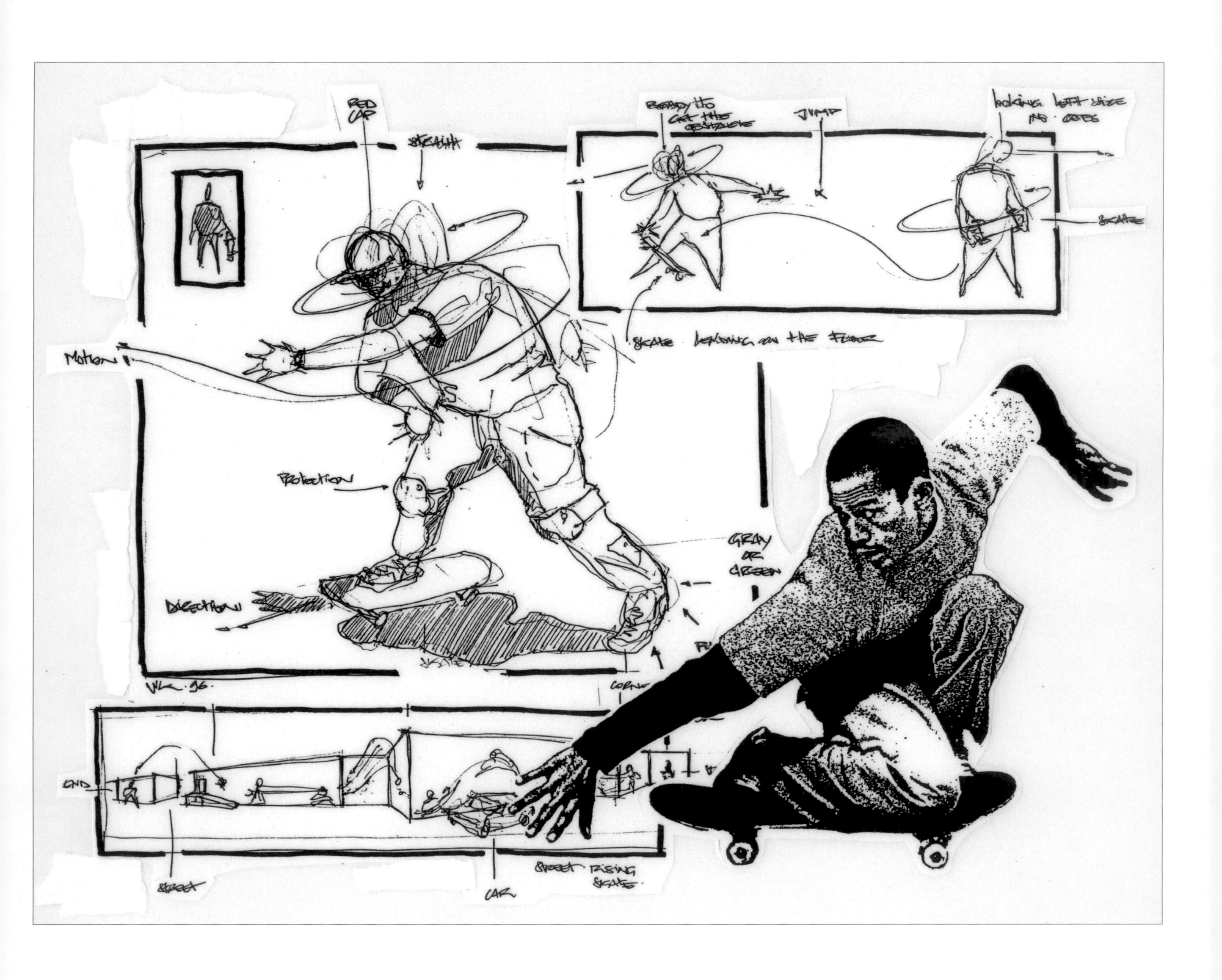

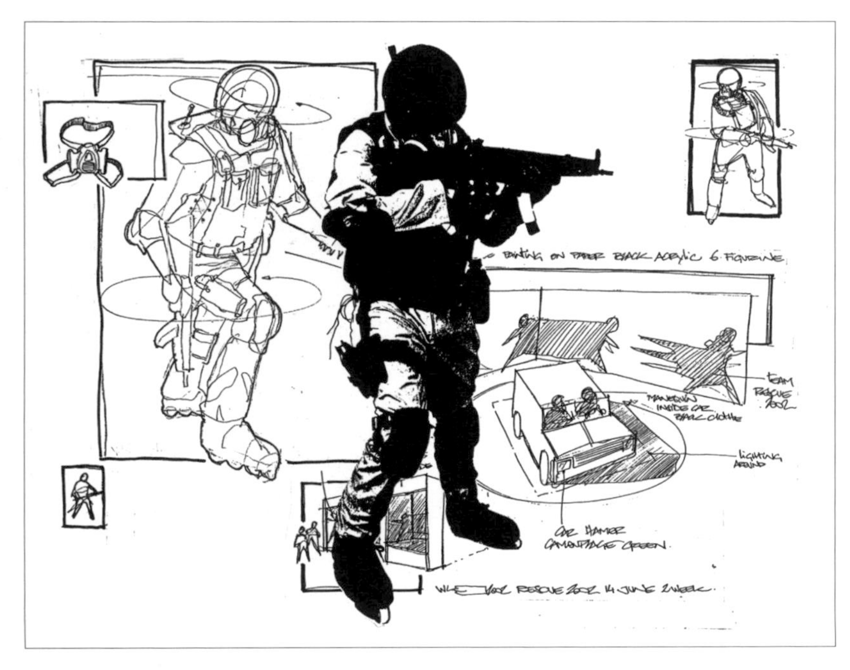

Harry Jumondji 100% urban skate (top) • Anti terrorism rescue team 2002 (bottom left) • Chase of businessman 1996 (bottom right)

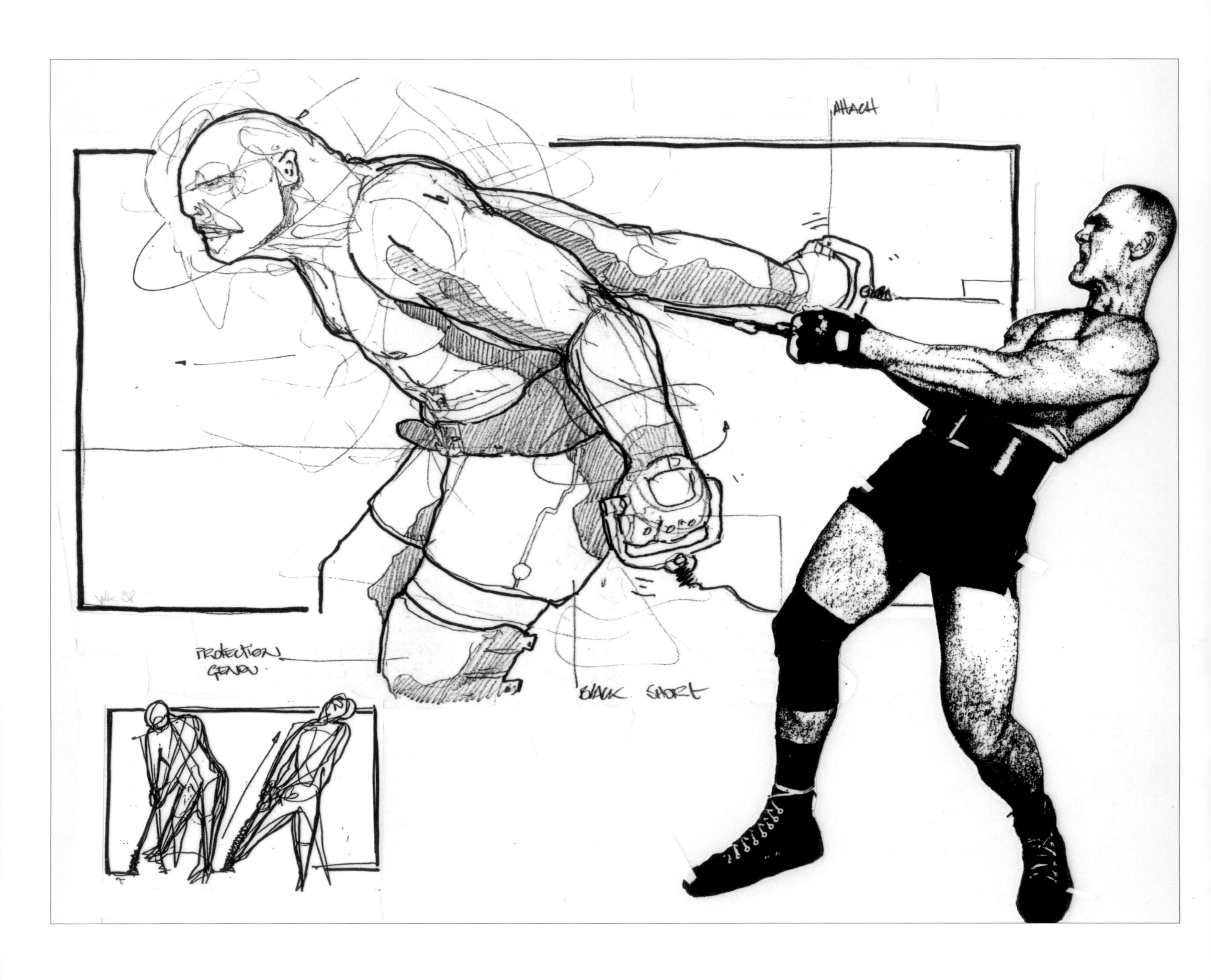

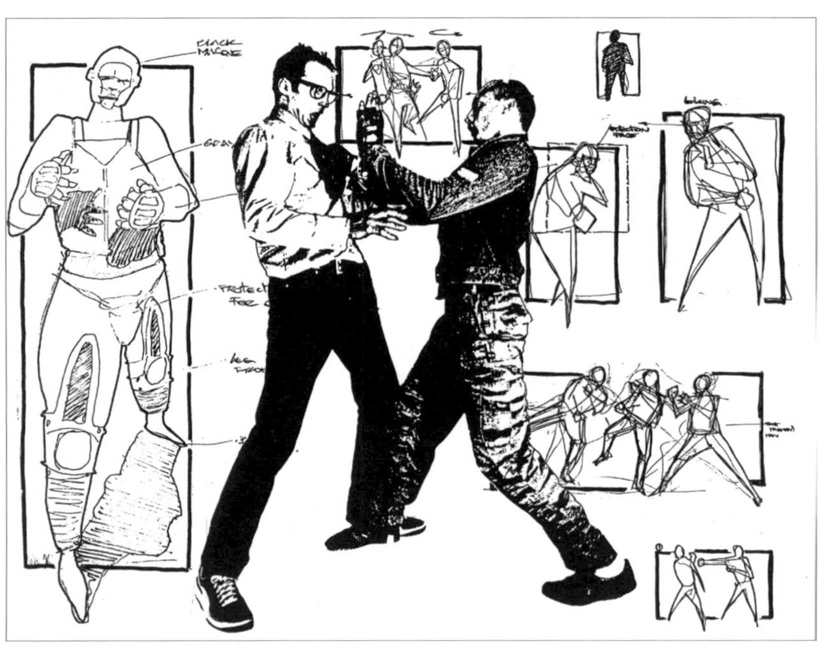

Man with power (top) • Downtown Chinatown attack of the businessman 1998 (bottom left) • Urban racing bike (bottom right)

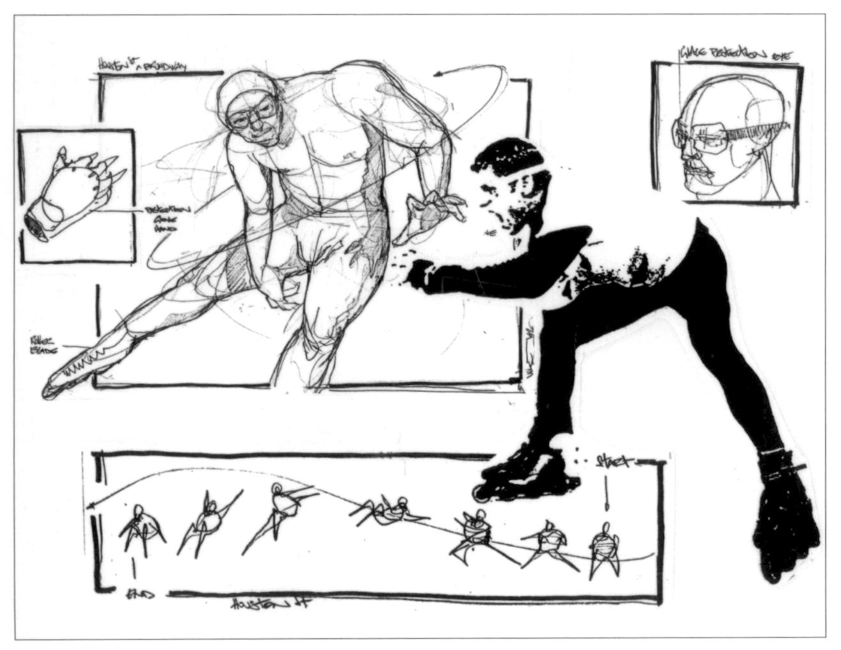

The ultimate spy (top) • Storyboard of roller blade in motion, Houston and Broadway (bottom left) • Escape through office window (bottom right)

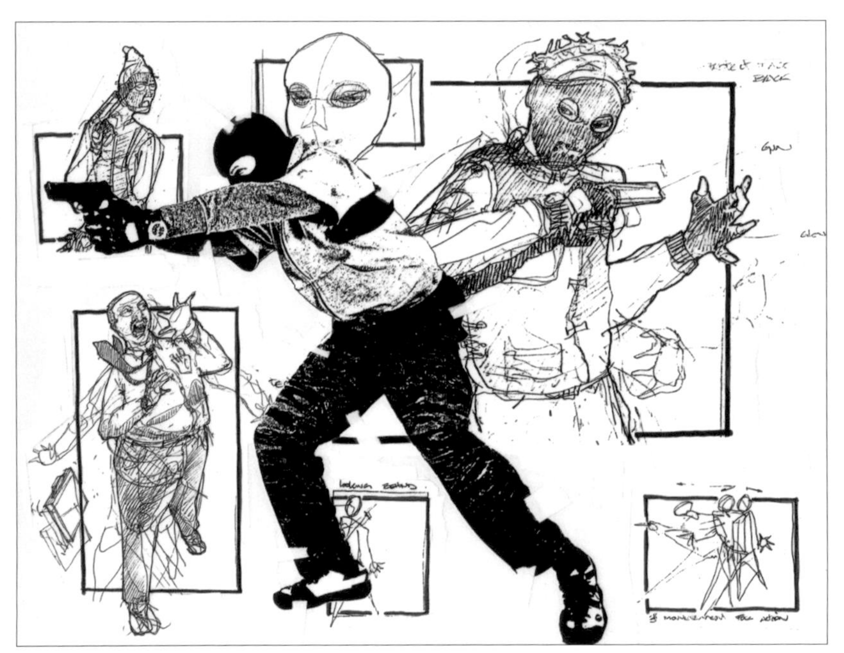

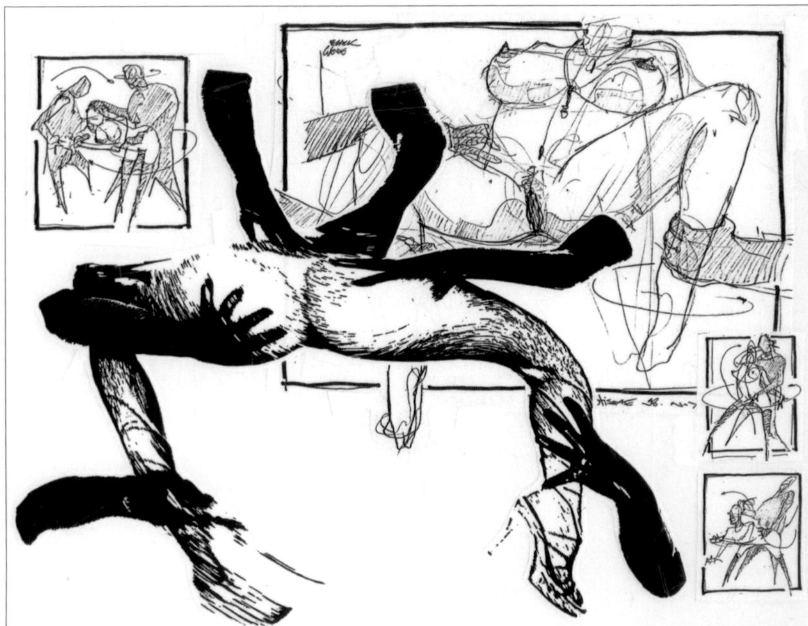

Impact 2000: Evaluation of the impact of a punch (top) • Set up of different angles for the chase of businessman (bottom left) • Motion of sex (bottom right)

Japanese fighter, Pride

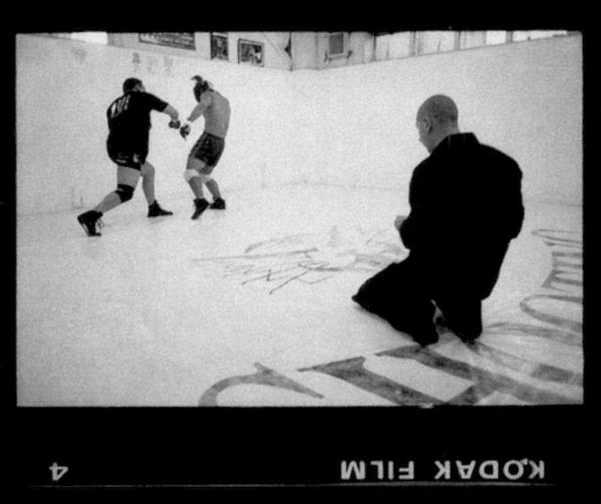

New York Times double page 2005

WKINTERACT NYC 05

New York Times double page 2005

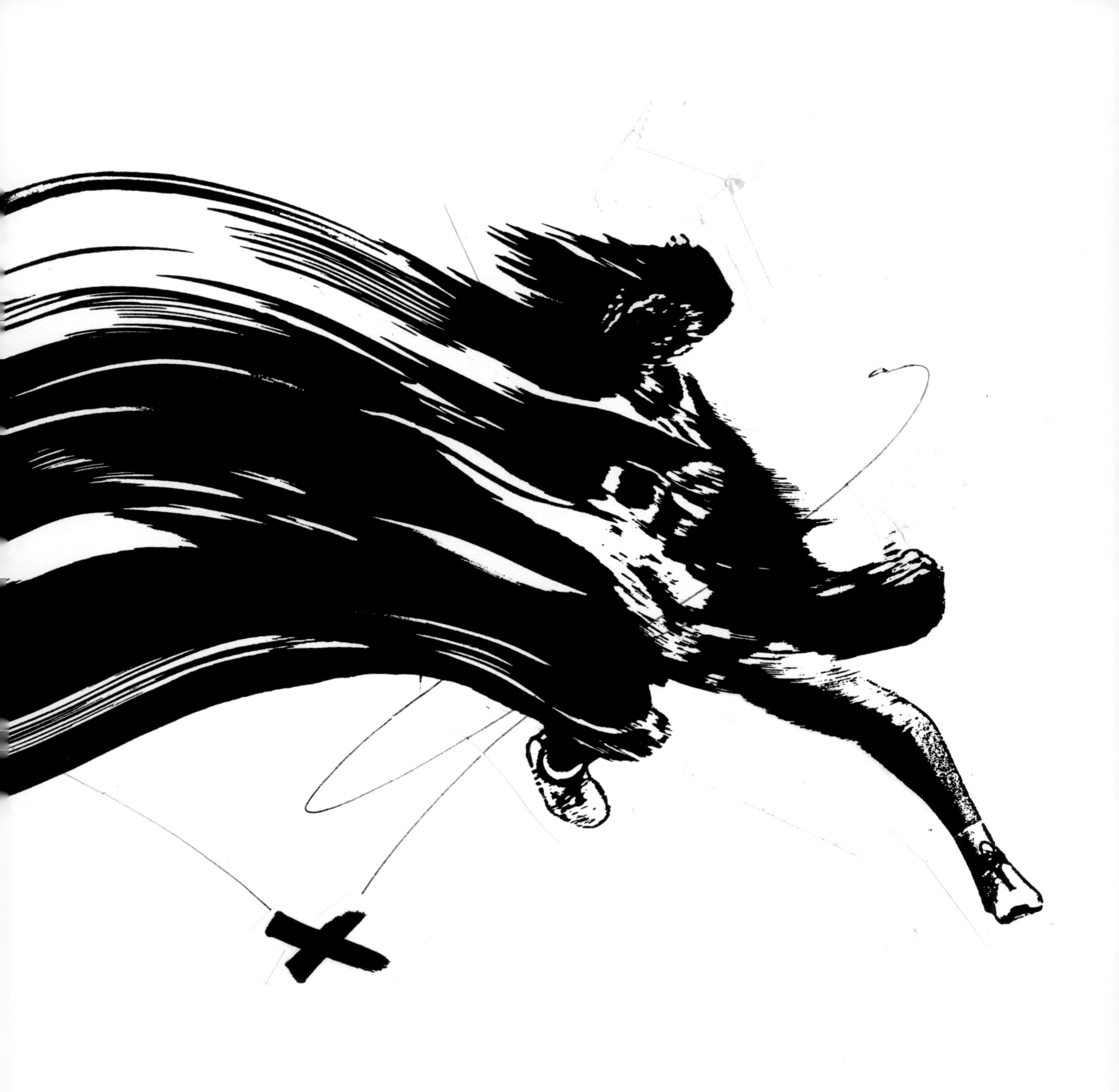

URBAN STREET 2004 NYC WK INTERACT DOWNTON LOWER EAST - SIDE

Characteristic tagger motion radius

Amplified tagger motion radius

JUNE ONE
KUMA

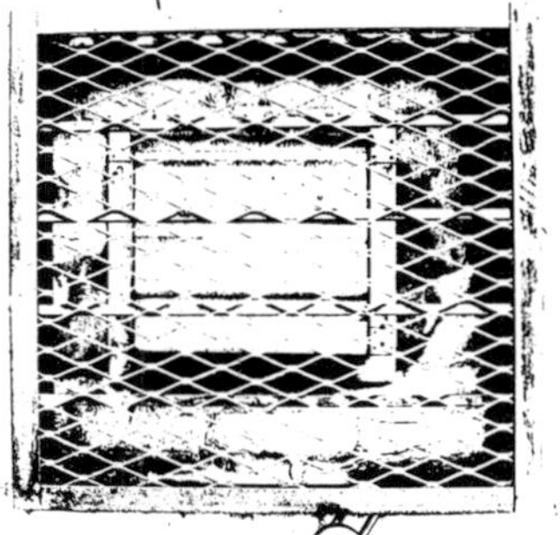
NO
PARKING
ANY
TIME
TOW AWAY
ZONE
ILLEGALLY PARKED AND
UNAUTHORIZED VEHICLES AT:
WILL BE TOWED AT
VEHICLE OWNER'S EXPENSE
AUTORAMA
(212) 222-1630

RAM

TAG
street NYC - 04

WISE PINK
KUMA
TEXAS
SNACH
NECKFACE
SHEPARD - OBEY
ASMA
CASPO
IRAK CREW
SACER
OJAS
KR
RAMBO
CLAW
AMASE
META
D
323
FAILE
FADE
FANTA
SETHEK
IRON
TWIST

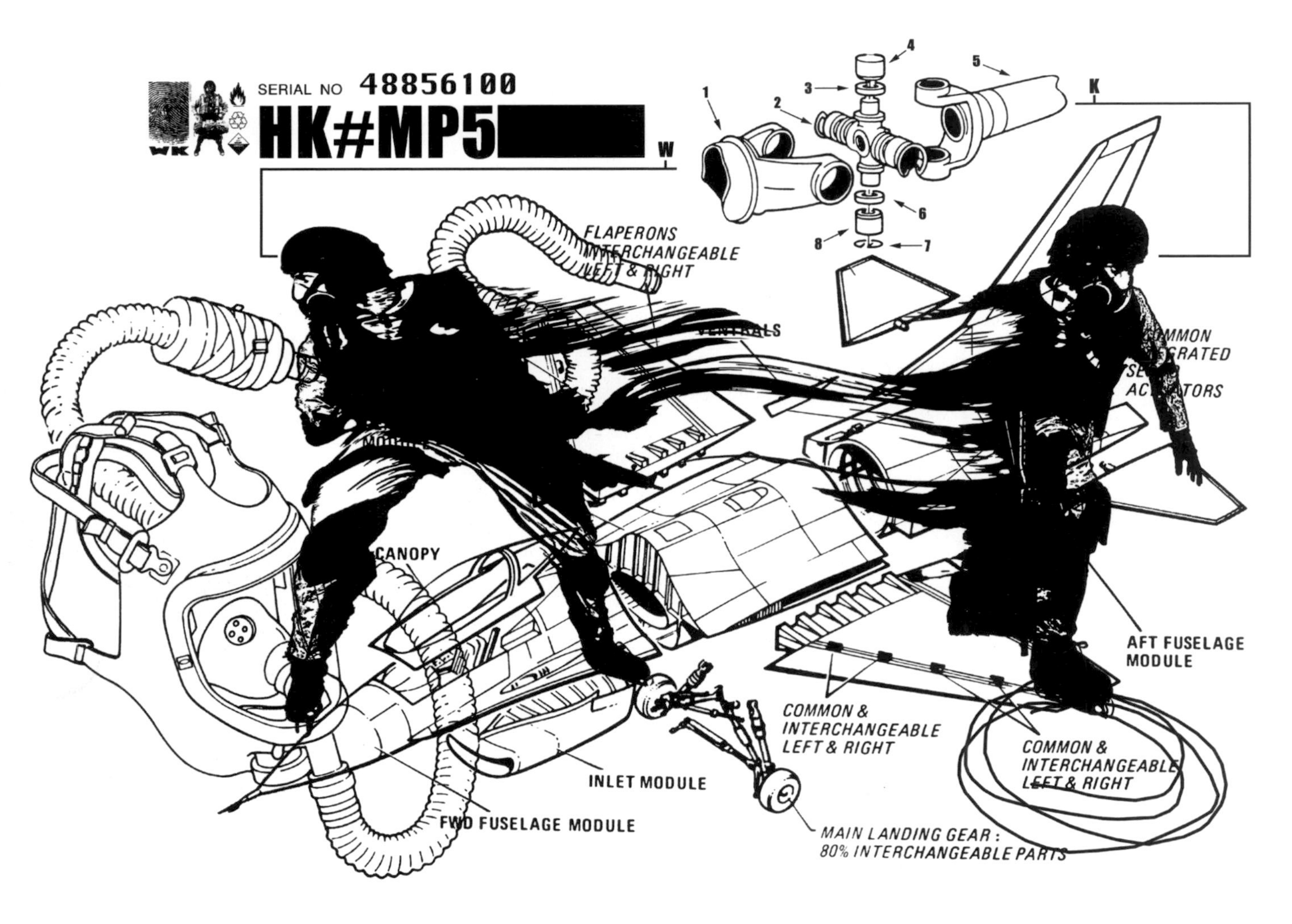

Rescue Force 2002 (top) • NYC struggle (bottom)

RT
SPLIT POST
4 NOTCHES
RESCUE-TEAM : ELITE COUNTERTERRORIST FORCE
FIGURE C #009530228*

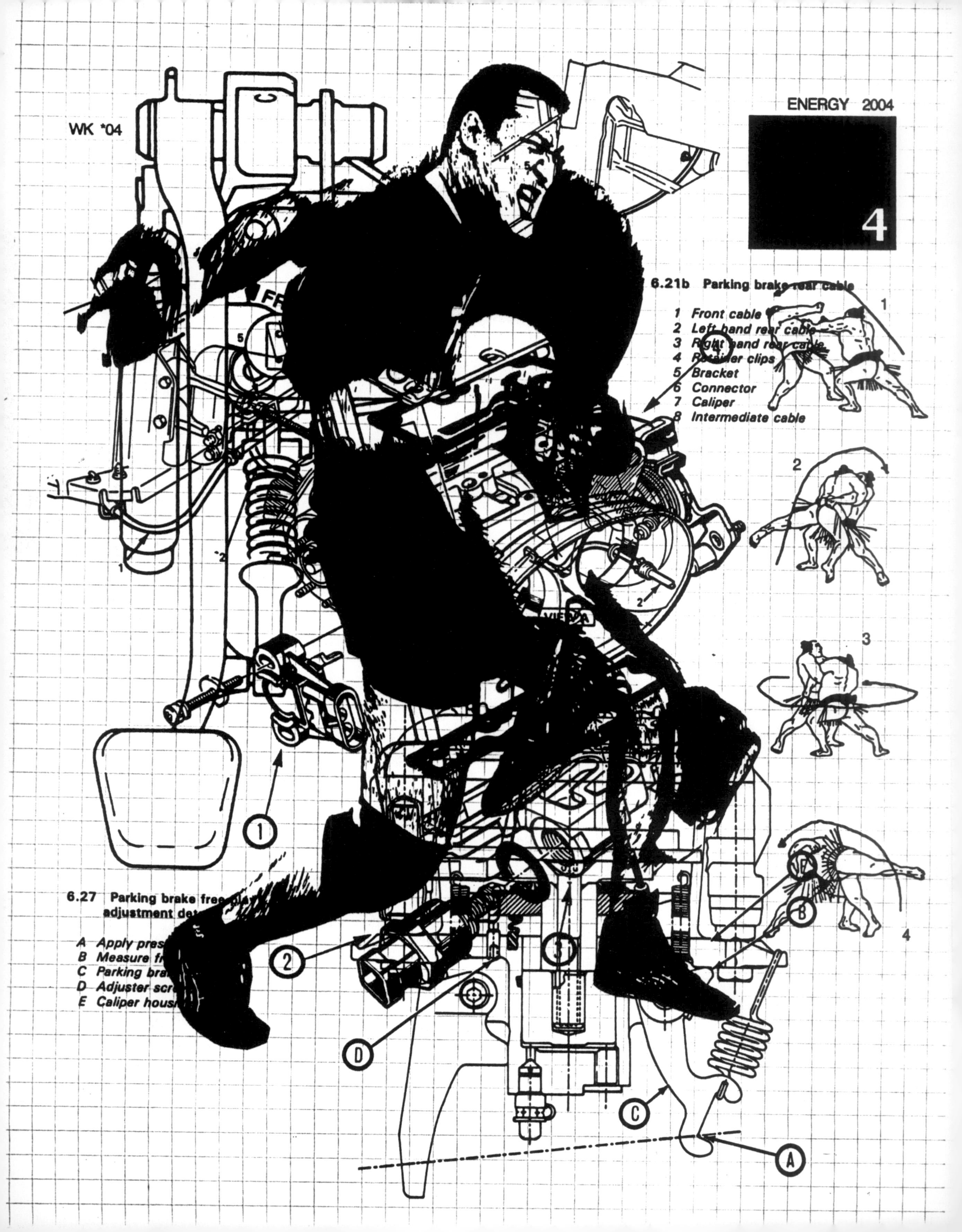
WK '04
ENERGY 2004
4
6.21b Parking brake rear cable
1 Front cable
2 Left hand rear cable
3 Right hand rear cable
5 Bracket
6 Connector
7 Caliper
8 Intermediate cable
6.27 Parking brake free
adjustment
A Apply pres
B Measure
C Parking bra
D Adjuster scr
E Caliper hous
1
2
3
4
A
B
C
D

178
Chapter 10 Suspension and steering systems
9.13 Use a chisel to knock out
10.4a Front
balljoint groove aligned with center of control arm boss
2 Hydraulic puller and adaptor for
Installation
4 Install the new balljoint using the same
of the control arm boss (see illustrations).
5 Place the new dust boot over the balljoint
clips (see Section 11).
6 Install the control arm as described i
10 Control arm balljoint – removal and installation
Refer to illustrations 10.2,
Removal
1 Remove the
W@*
WK2004

Art piece acrylic on wood and aluminium with punch bag for applied experience (top) • Acrylic on canvas, 5'x6'

Art piece based on recycled street objects, 7'x5' (top) • Art piece acrylic on wood and aluminium with training gun and target for applied experience

Camouflage, Acrylic on canvas, 5'x6'

Art piece based on recycled street objects, 5'x4'

Splashed acrylic on canvas 7'x5'

Art piece acrylic on wood and aluminium, 5'x6'

Art piece based on recycled objects 2005, 8'x5' (top) • Work in progress at Studio 101

*05
*05

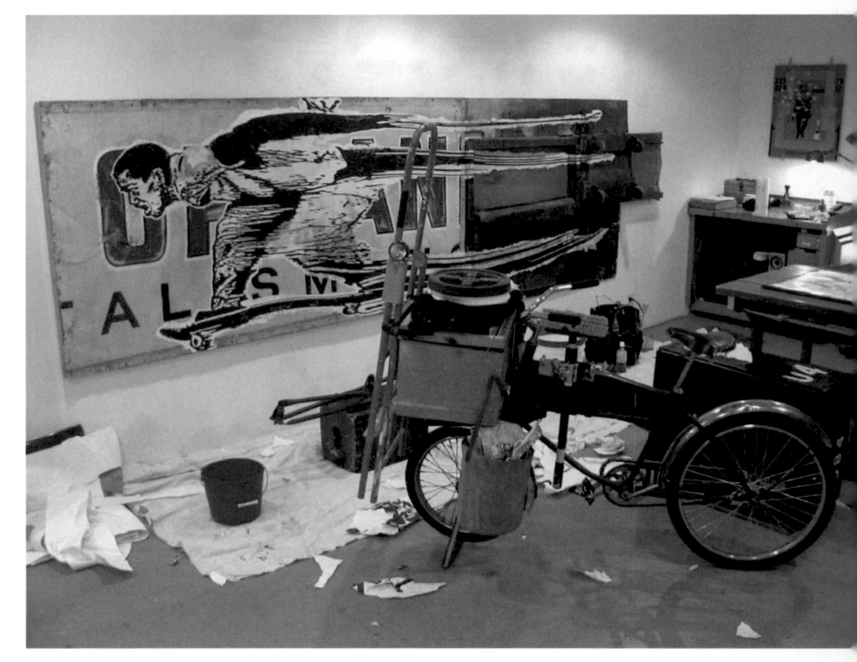

Interact Us street collaboration 2003, 101 Stanton St

大和魂
05

Placement of 9 yellow panels for 24 hours, 101 Stanton storefront

禁止
6時
渋谷区

SIGN HERE

NIGHT REGULATION
INCLUDING SUNDAY
ADA FABRICS
MOVED TO
ALEX FABRICS
155 ORCHARD ST

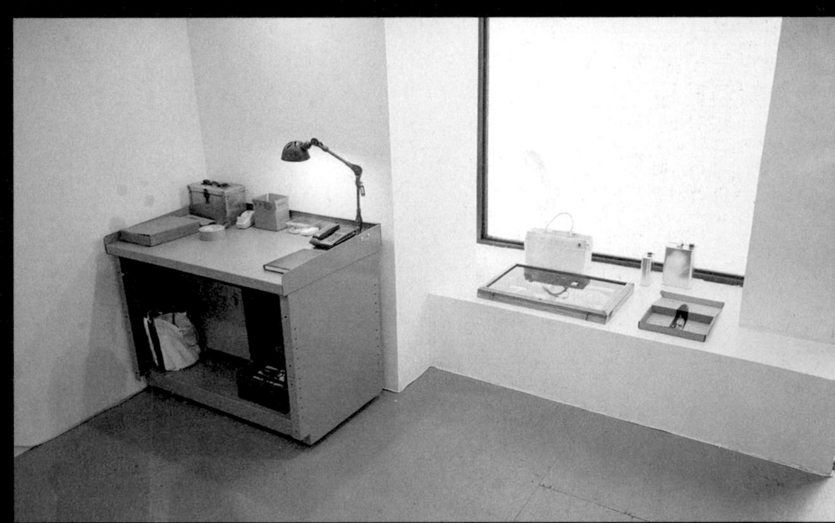

TOILET BOYS
PETER
SIMONEZ
BEST WISHES
CHRISSCOTT
DARIUS JONES
TURK
ZAPATA
Fumika
Hiroko
ASAKO
FAILE

Interactive secret door at opening of Studio 101, 2000

T-shirt de-fragmentation project Collaboration 101 with Yael

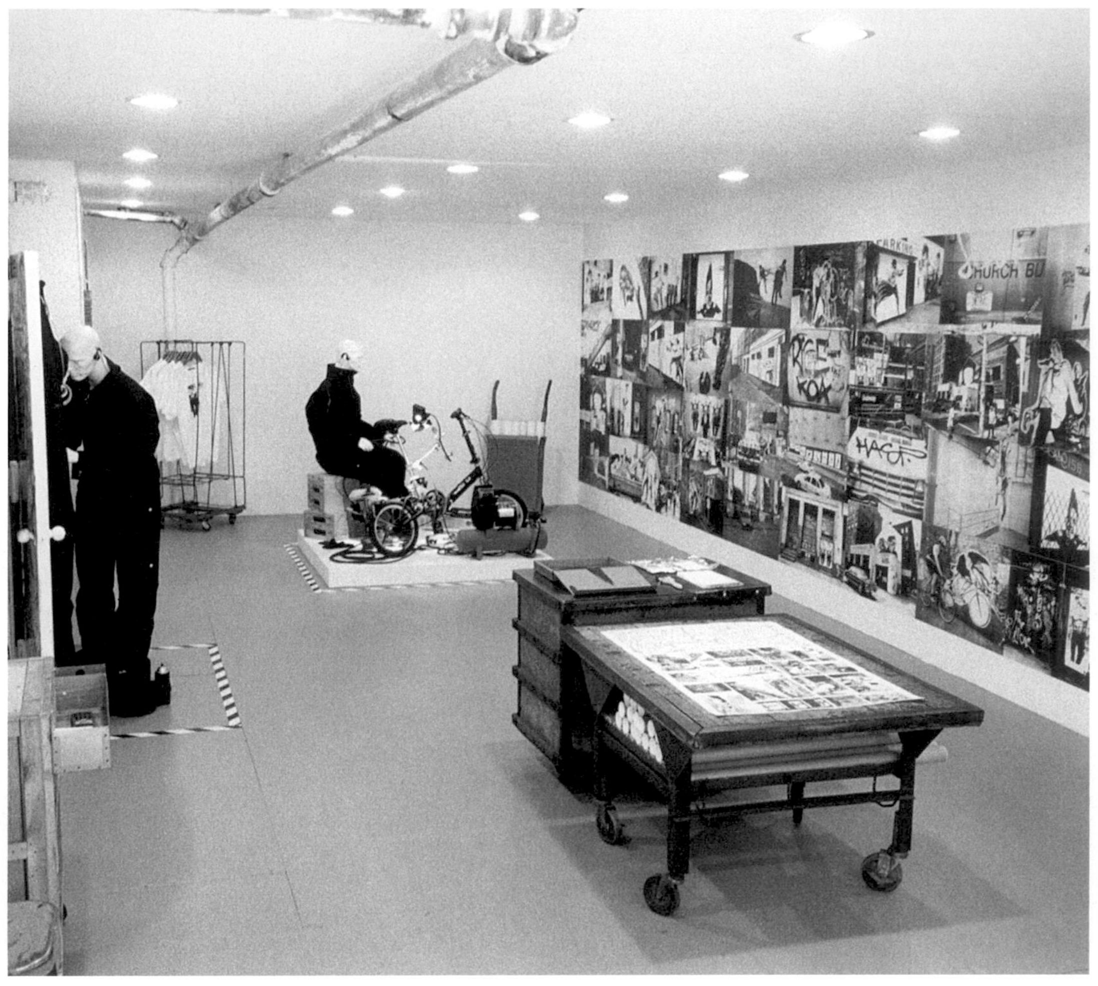

Tool man 2002 at Studio 101

Master Lee martial art sequence setup

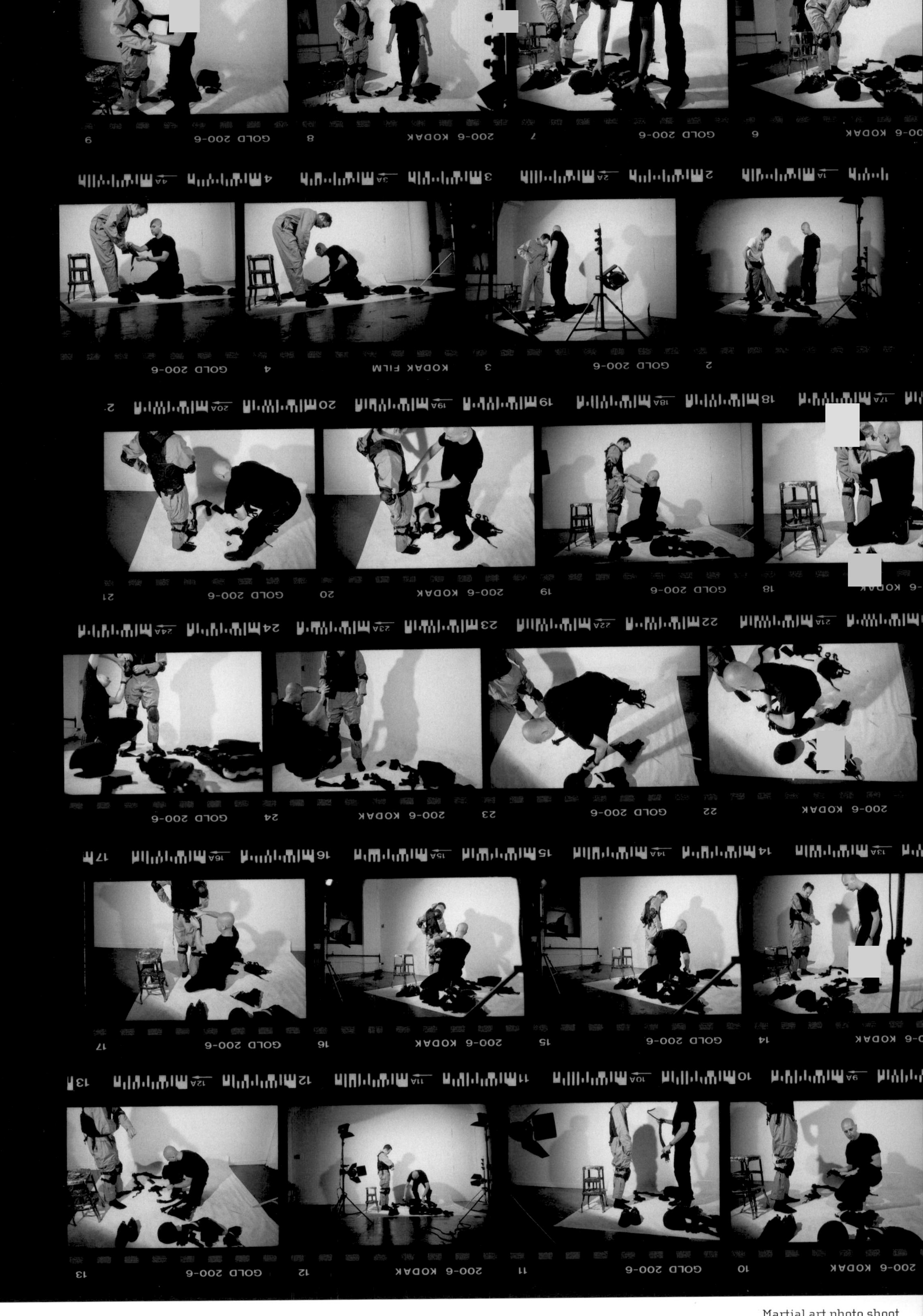

WK fingerprint camouflage helmet (top left) • WK fingerprint camouflage hockey mask (top right) • WK camo spray can (bottom left) • WK camo skate board (bottom left)

WK camo mickey mouse

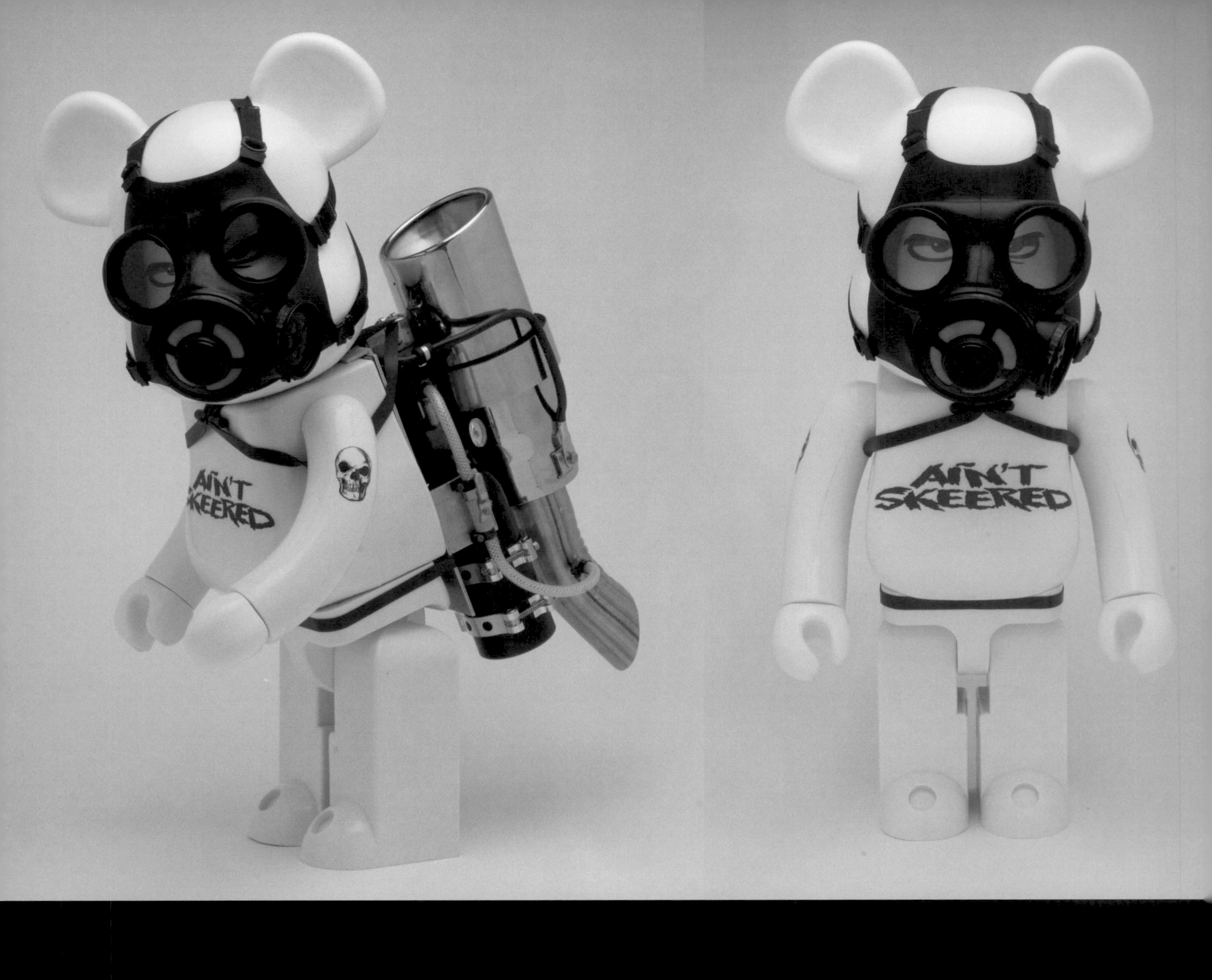

WK rocket. Collaboration with Medicom Toy

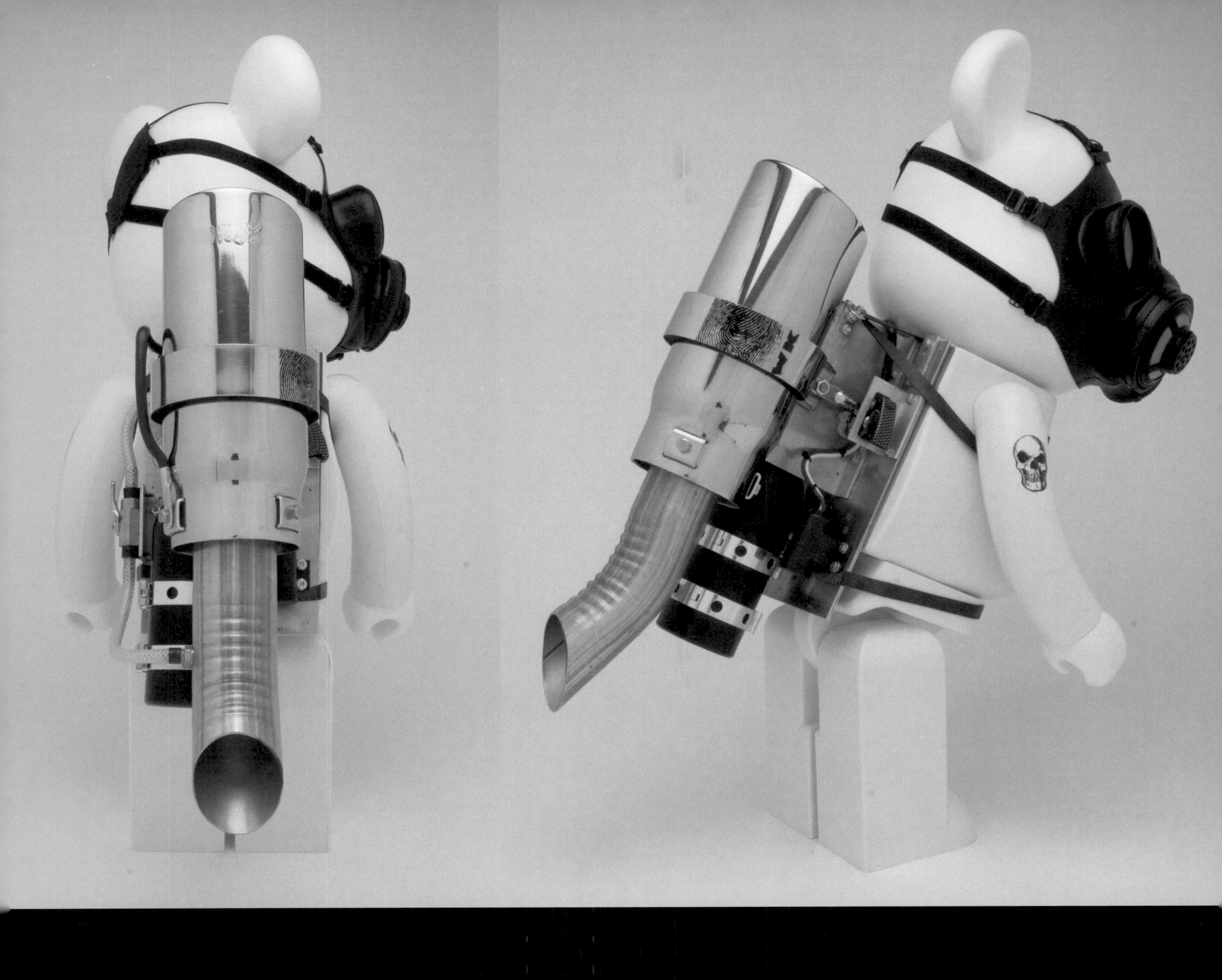

Accumulation of recycled packaging materials

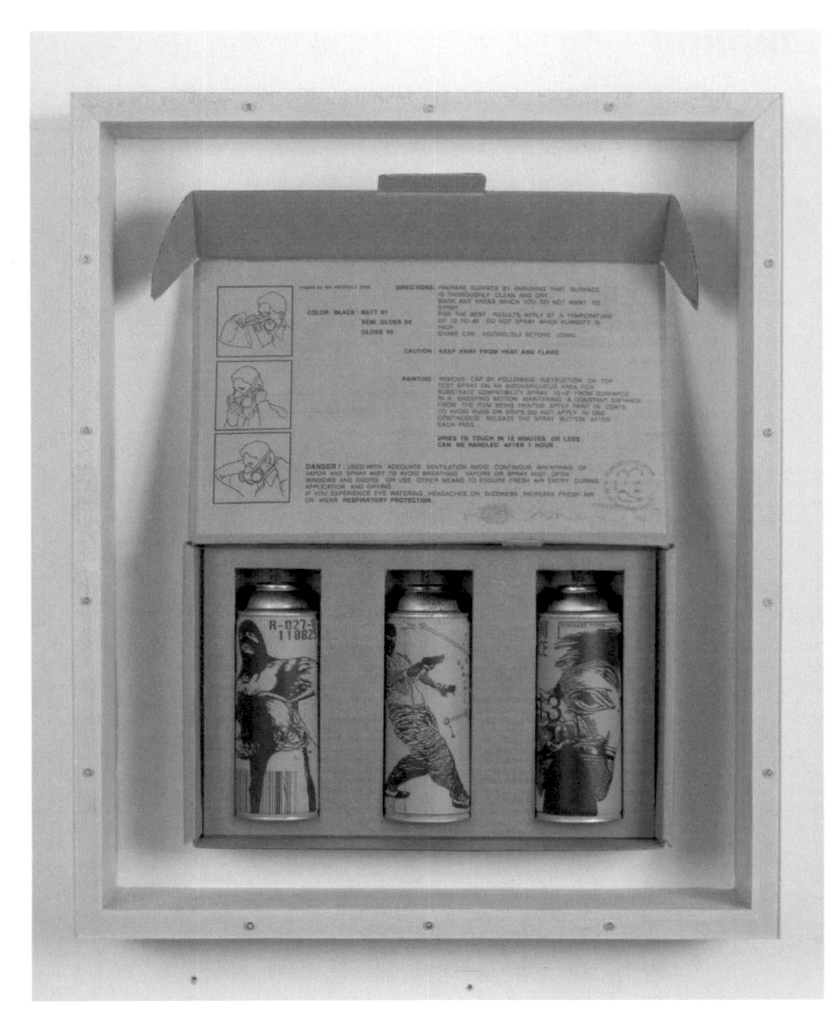

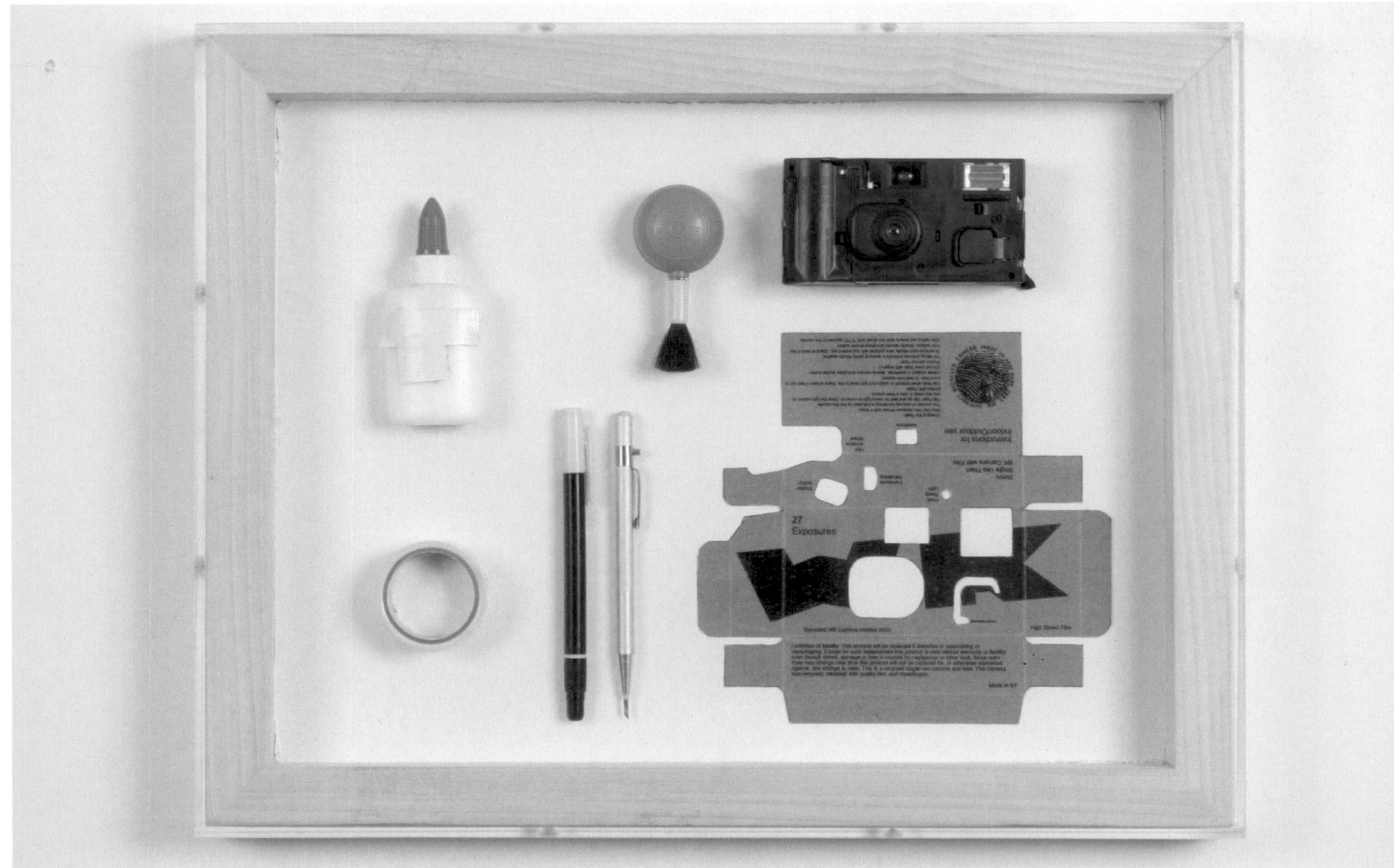

Recycled spray can display (top left) • Principle of camouflage demonstrated on various objects (top right) • Create your own recycled objects packaging kit (bottom)

Principle of camouflage demonstrated on various objects, black

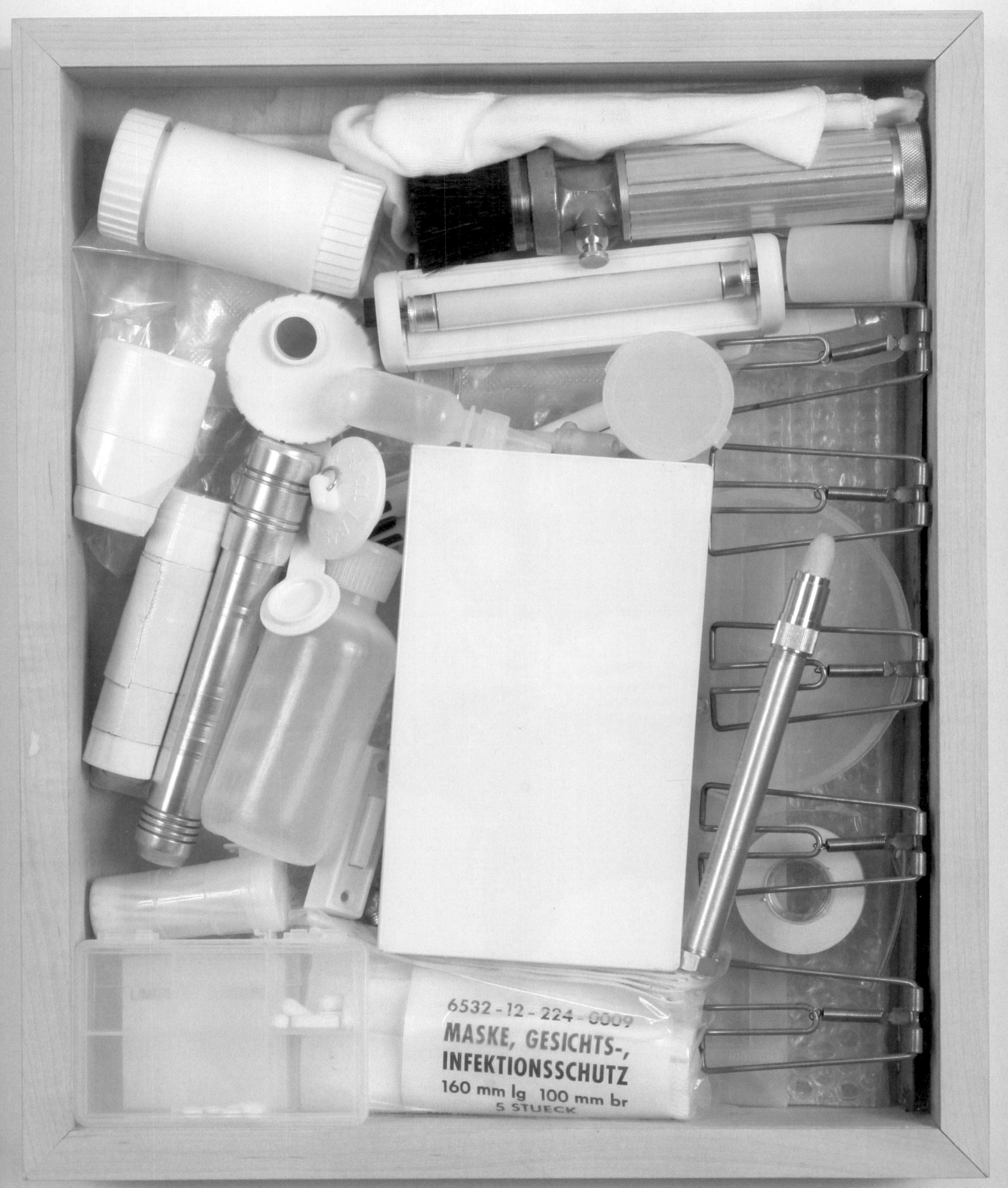

Principle of camouflage demonstrated on various objects, white

CORROSIVE

WK artwork stamps

Street survival kit at Lower East Side Winter morning

Mr. Camo and his belongings

Nighttime bombing with purpose-optimized vehicle

Bombing vehicle complete

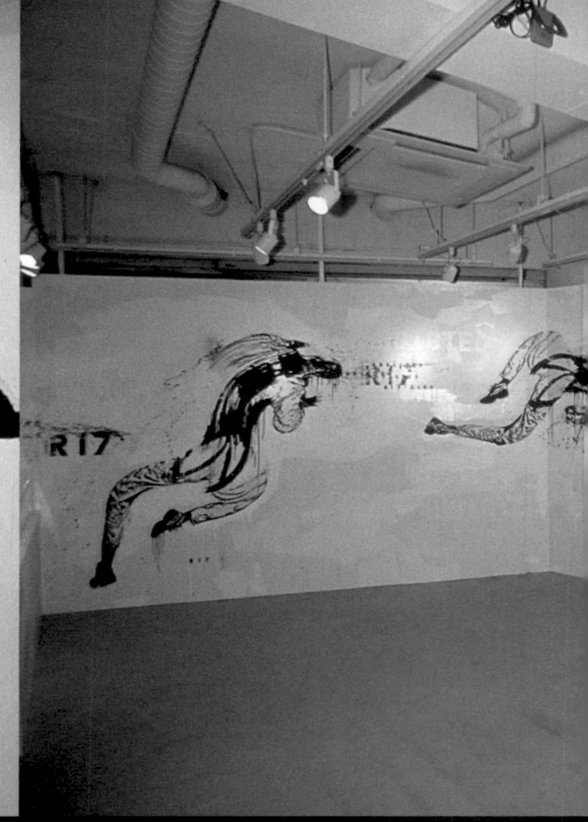

YAMAHA

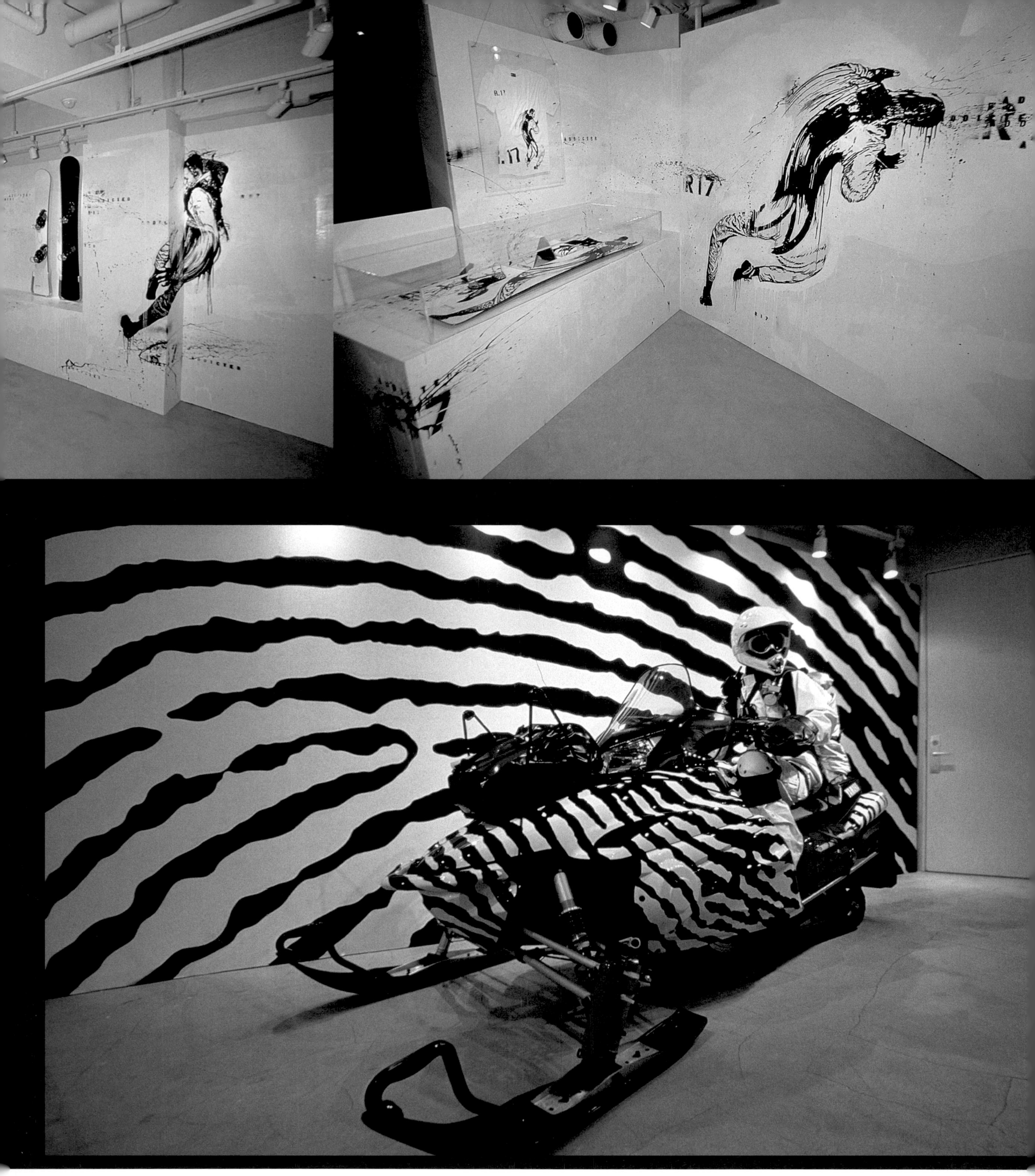

R.17#ADDICTED
R.17#ADDICTED
R.17
R.17

Project Fox for VW, Copenhagen

NO PARKING ANY TIME
TOW AWAY ZONE

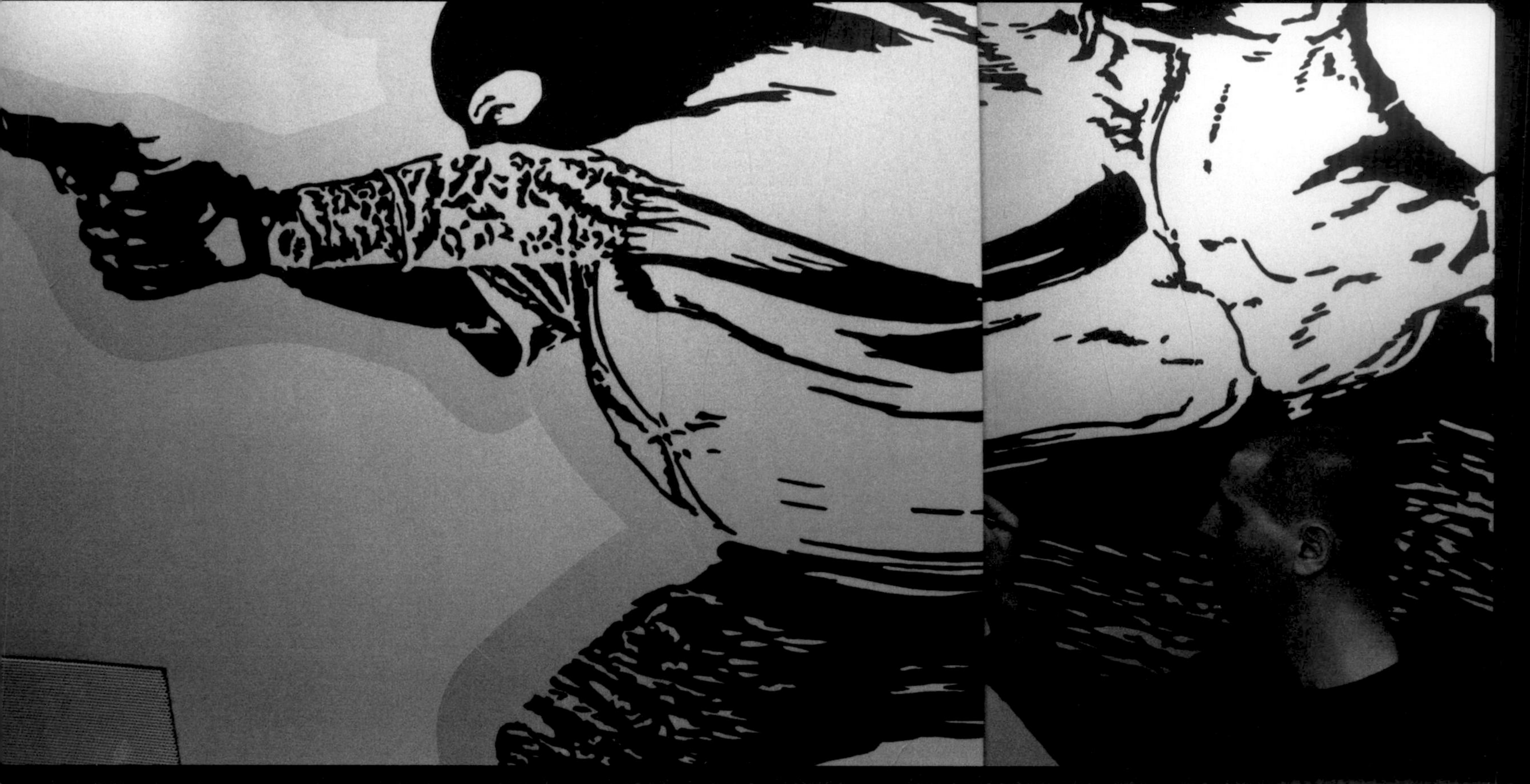

Collaboration with BMW at Patricia Dorffman Gallery

Sexy Beast, Berlin

SEX
SEX
XX2
SEX
SEX
XX2
SEX
SEX

Dazed and Confused Gallery installation

Runaway Stairway Sydney, Australia 2003

44

PENNZOIL
REGINA
SERVICE
CENTER
WK INTERACT WK INTERACT WK INTERACT WK INTERACT
RESCUE2002

by owner
Tel: 718 721-4882
LIFETIME
MUFFLERS
custom muffler specialists
REGINA AUTO SERVICE CENTER
OFFICIAL
STATE OF NEW YORK
MOTOR VEHICLE
INSPECTION STATION
ACDelco
BATTERIES

USMC
LIFT HERE
MAG-36
LIFT HERE
DY 205Z

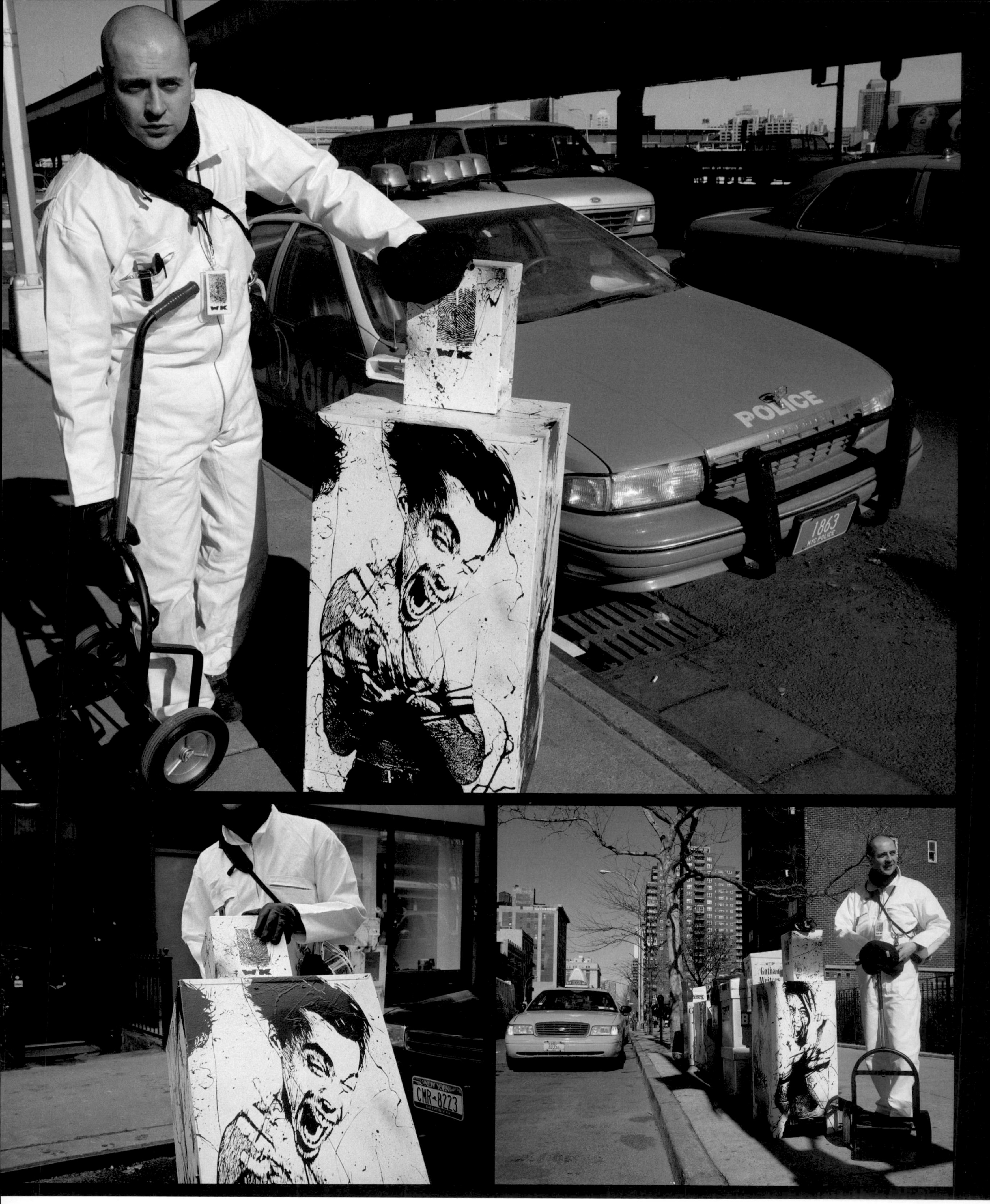

WK propaganda stand

ATM
USA TODAY
CIGARETTES
COLD DRINKS
COFFEE & TEA
ATM INSIDE
METROCARDS
FILM &
BATTERIES
SOLD HERE

ONE WAY
NEW YORK POST

NEW YORK
CMR 822

WK propaganda stand

3L92
Gotham
Writers'
FREE
DAILY
am
New York
Down-
town

Human Motion

Manhattan Bridge

Rollerblade on the corner of Houston and Broadway

Working on the corner of Houston and Broadway (top) • Lower East Side, Rivington St (bottom)

Target in Japan (top) • Businessman Lafayette and Prince St, 1993 (bottom)

Businessman Lafayette and Prince St, 1993

Climber Lower East Side

Bleeker St

BOGA NE: A ne Thera y fo
Chem al Dep dence
minates P ysic Withdraw
and Inte Drug Cravi
avior.
WKO4

The Tagger, Rivington St

The Tagger, Wooster St

The Tagger

WK04

Sexy Dream, Paris

RONA HARTNER
Voyage tzigane
EN TOURNÉE

Trapped in SoHo

Businessman Lafayette and Prince St, 1993

Houston Street

Series of 182 target posters placed all over Manhattan

220
BAR CiCHETTi 220

Series of 182 target posters placed all over Manhattan

251
-0375
NVR

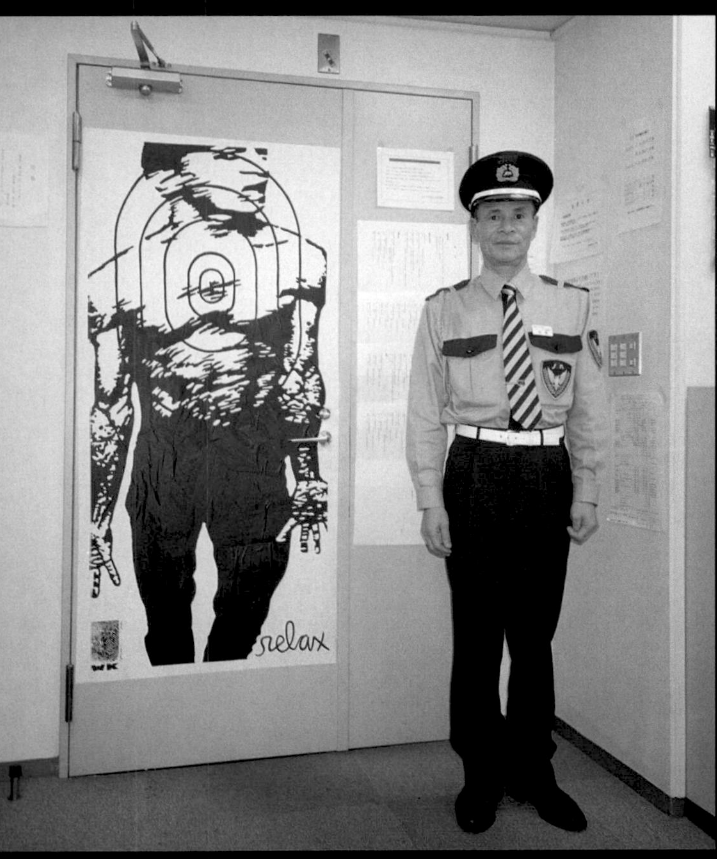

Series of 182 target posters placed all over Manhattan

DAVID SILVERIA
NEW
Gentle Touch
Car Wash
24 Hours
22.83
Maximum/+Tax
Enter 5-10:00AM
Early Bird
13.53
Out By 8PM/+Tax
Subway
MetroCard
MetroCard
Vending Machines
At This Station
Self Serve
No Smoking
Stop Engine
NWC
BLAZE

Pose on Lafayette (top) • The Tagger

Running killer in the UK

PENA

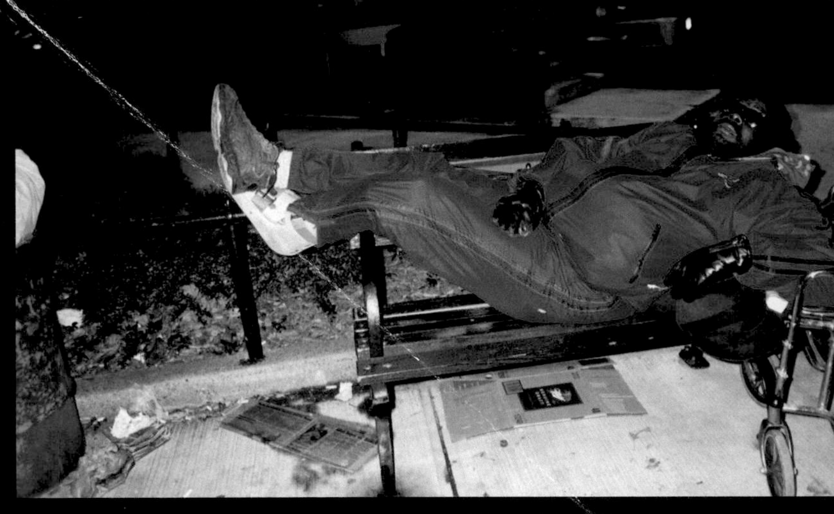

MOVING
SUPPLIES
BUY-RENT
WHOLESALE RETAIL
Mendon
LEASING
RENTAL
USED TRUCKS
FOR SALE
RENT - BUY

OPEN
24hrs
BAJWA
AUTO
BODY WORK
OPEN 24
NYC TAXI
4M11

475-6233

VEHICLES

New York City

Phone booth

First poster installation using corner to create dimensions in motion, NYC, 1993

FOR SALE
212 226-4322
Tel. 212 406-0112
The Corner Restaurant
925-9360
to TAKE OUT 6AM TO 11AM
MOVERS
2854

Crashed messenger, Dan

Fight on Ludlow

Lower East Side, Harry Jumonji, 100% skate

Lower East Side, Ludlow St

Lower East Side, Rivington St

122

Chinese homeless man, Manhattan (top) • Wintertime, Coney Island (bottom)

Limousine Driver, Manhattan (top) • Summertime, Bryant Park (bottom)

Canal St and Broadway

DRI

Lafayette and Prince (top)

Phone Booth Spring and Lafayette (top)

REGINA AUTO SERVIC CENTER
REGINA SERVICE CENTER
NEW YORK STATE INSPECTION
←PARKING
5Y59

Crosby St 1992

Parking Soho (top) • Assassin on Lafayette (bottom)

NYC struggle on Lafayette

NYC struggle on Lafayette

Mrs. K, UK

Impact 2000 above WK Studio 101

Smile of Alek Wek

REGINA AUTO SERVICE CENTER
COMPLETE AUTO REPAIRS · AUTO & BODY PAINTING · TOWING
LIFETIME
AIR CONDITIONING

ARKING
PARK
FOR SOHO LITTLE ITALY PUCK BLDG
& BROADWAY SHOPPING
MOTOR VEHICLE
REPAIR SHOP
NY97

Garagedoor on Ludlow St

R-027-079-A
1108257
NEW YORK USA
4
0359
HEADACHE
27003541

Street installation Sydney

Street installation Sydney

002
001

Street installation Sydney

002
002
002

Attack on Lafayette 2004

WK04
o4
#3789004
985

Attack on Lafayette 2004

13
#3789004
33
#3789004

Attack on Lafayette 2004

Suitcase with refillable spray gun: 3 ink bottles, portable air pressure system, replacement caps, fat ink marker, ink brush

Portable mini stencil case

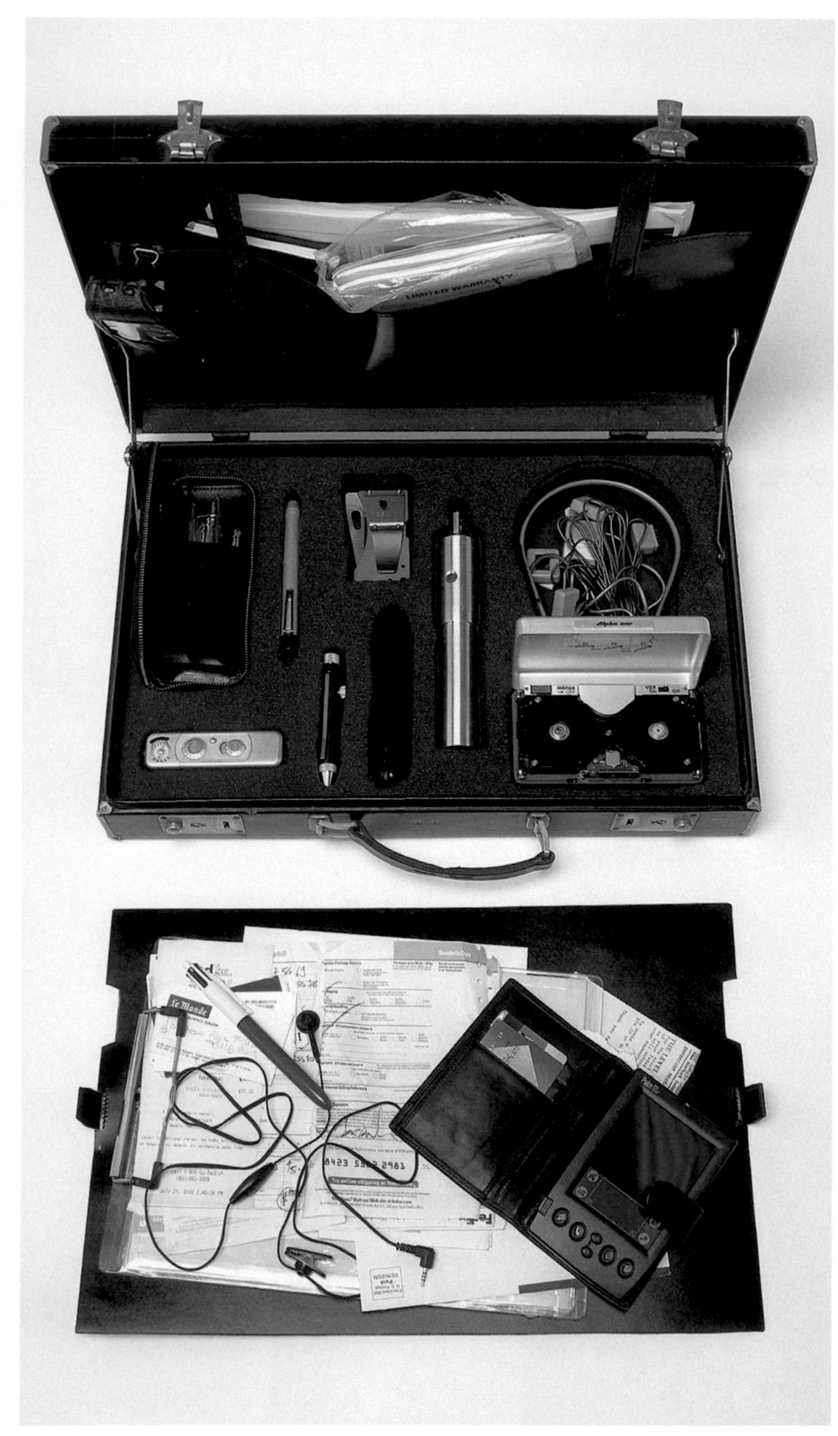

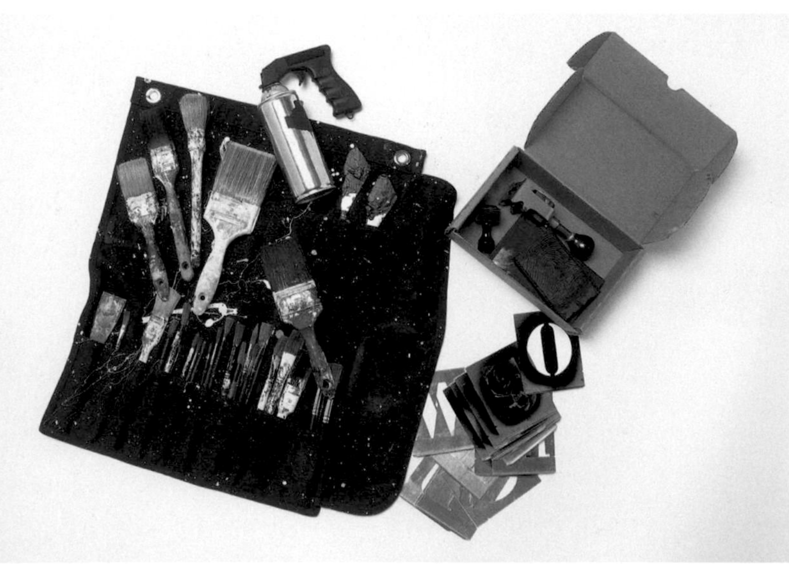

Spy business case kit: recording system, suitcase lock smith tools including drill, minox spy camera (top left) • False bottom suitcase traveling kit with hidden black foam compartments for diverse tools: stickers, spray can, marker brush and refill, stamp, mini marker (top right) • Painting tool (bottom)

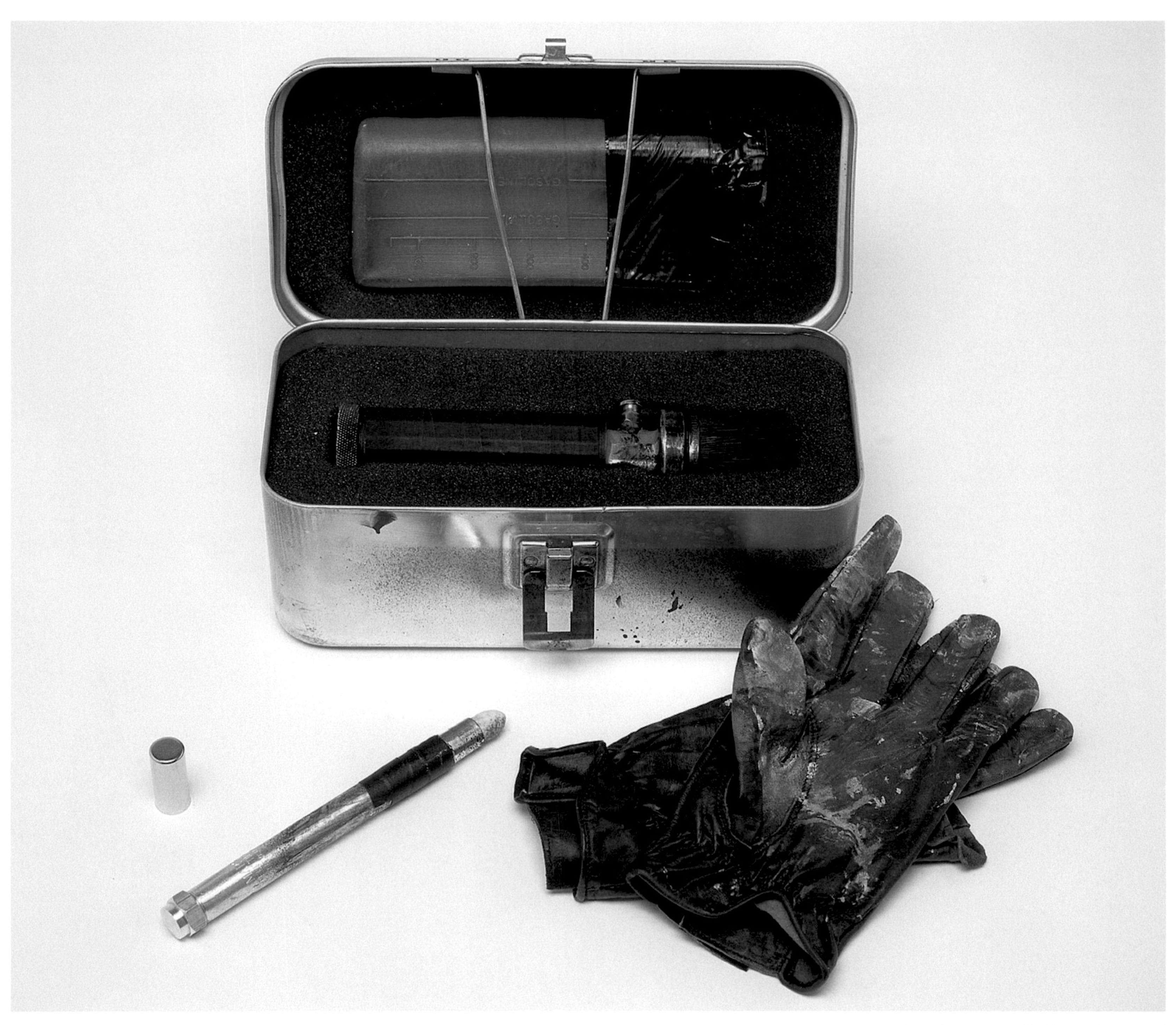

Lunch box containing marker brush and ink refill (top) • Collaboration with Hello Kitty, Kitty Kit spy case (bottom)

Bike outfit: helmet, spray can holders on back waistband, small German army back pack, gluing extension brush, small aluminum note book, walkie-talkie phone, mini cap, poster bag for A16 posters, small hip bag containing spray can, marker and stickers, WK tape and tape holder

Nocturnal propaganda complete gear: outfit with spray can holder straps different levels for quick access, russian night vision, climbing rope, cutter for fences and locks, oxygen spray can extension allcwing for longer spraying, bag containing projector, extension cord, WK tape, marker and brush, hybrid city/climbing shoes, ammunition jacket holding 6 spray cans, black face mask, watch

Portable shelter for urban street stencil activist: bottomless cardboard box, generic gas mask for spraying from inside the box, aluminum stencil sheet, comfortable and solid footwear (top) • New York fashion week photographer kit: edwin shoes, wig, calve leather gloves, remote button, polaroid camera and lenses, suitcase containing custom made spray unit made of car tire air pump to allow infinite spraying

Urban camouflage kit based on garbage bags: gloves, double spray can, black hood, mini skate board, bag to carry spray can (top) • Fake handicapped homeless kit for both, daytime and nighttime camouflage the wheelchair street level allowing to tag on cars: wig, moustache, glasses, headphones containing radio transmitting set, knee splints , wheel chair gloves, small hip bag containing spray can, bag for stencils to be attached on the side of the wheelchair

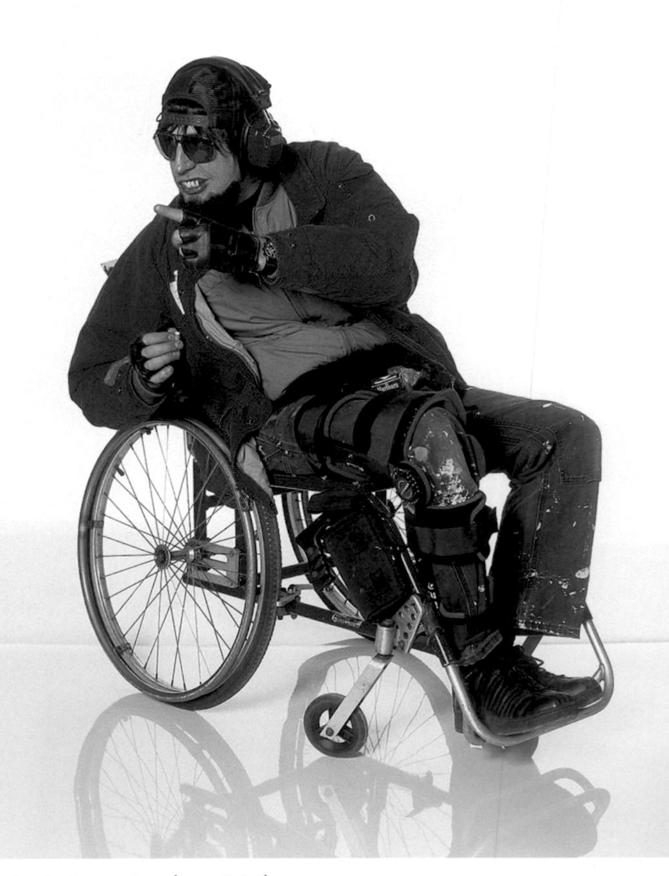

Daytime camouflage Grand Central Station regular business man (top left) • New York fashion week photographer (top right) • Garbage bag camouflage applied (bottom left) • Demonstrating handicapped outfit (bottom right)

Complete gear fitted front and back (top) • Final outfit standing (bottom left) • Shelter applied (bottom right)

Pliable bike with engine for long distance activities (top) • WK fingerprint stamp shoes (bottom)

Nighttime long distance equipment with folding engine mini bicycle

WK Interact: Exterior - Interior Act 2

Edited by Robert Klanten and Hendrik Hellige

Scan + Color Reproduction: Czech & Partner, Berlin
Production Management: Janine Milstrey and Martin Bretschneider
Printed by Graphicom Srl, Vicenza

Interview: Isabel Kirsch (Adam Nagata and Evan Baggs: thanks for editing)

Made in Europe.

Bibliographic information published by Die Deutsche Bibliothek. Die Deutsche Bibliothek lists this publication
in the Deutsche Nationalbibliografie; detailed bibliographic data is available in the Internet at http://dnb.ddb.de.

ISBN 3-89955-070-6

For more information please check
www.die-gestalten.de.

Respect copyright, encourage creativity!